To my good friend
HANK

Love
J. Patah Gaylor
2006

A FLAG AT HALF-MAST

A Personal Account of the Attack on America

J. PATCH GUGLIELMINO
A DISASTER RELIEF
WORKER

Bloomington, IN Milton Keynes, UK

authorHOUSE

AuthorHouse™
1663 Liberty Drive, Suite 200
Bloomington, IN 47403
www.authorhouse.com
Phone: 1-800-839-8640

AuthorHouse™ UK Ltd.
500 Avebury Boulevard
Central Milton Keynes, MK9 2BE
www.authorhouse.co.uk
Phone: 08001974150

This book is a work of non-fiction. Unless otherwise noted, the author and the publisher make no explicit guarantees as to the accuracy of the information contained in this book and in some cases, names of people and places have been altered to protect their privacy.

First published by AuthorHouse 7/13/2006

ISBN: 1-4259-4196-6 (sc)

Library of Congress Control Number: 2006904871

Printed in the United States of America
Bloomington, Indiana

This book is printed on acid-free paper.

TO:

THE SILENT HEROES WHO SUPPORTED THE
POLICE, FIRE, AND RESCUE PERSONNEL
OF THE SEPTEMBER 11TH ATTACK ON AMERICA

THE LIGHT SHINES ON IN DARKNESS
A DARKNESS THAT DID NOT OVERCOME IT.
JOHN 1:8

ACKNOWLEDGMENTS

I wish to acknowledge my husband, Louis for his patience and support with this project and my two close friends Jeffry D. Levesque, MSW, LCSW-C, Red Cross Mental Health Specialist, and R. Kevin Rowell, Ph.D. Assoc. Professor of Psychology/Counseling, University of Central Arkansas, Red Cross Mental Health Specialist. A special thanks to Winfred Medin R.N. MA who is always there for me with her great sense of humor and constant encouragement. Michael Montgomery, LCSW, MFT, who has helped me wade through the pain of post-traumatic stress enabling me to finish this work, and to psychologist Marilyn Wooley and Mike Pool of the West Coast Post-Trauma Retreat in Inverness, California who gave me back my life so I could continue with my humanitarian work. Special thanks to E. B. Wood for editing this book.

Rev. James Hayes an incredibly courageous hero who generously shared his experiences and feelings to assist in the creation of this book, a man who has supported my journey toward healing, a man who ran toward disaster and not away from it.

Thanks to David Sinclair, General Manager of Spirit Cruises of New York/New Jersey who so willingly supplied me with information about their wonderful ship *The Spirit of New York* and their incredible participation in the relief efforts.

THE BEGINNING
11 September 2001 – Tuesday
5:46 a.m. Pacific Standard Time
Healdsburg, California

An indelible mark branded on our souls today a day that would be like no other, a day of fear and uncertainty, a day a war was born. The impact felt throughout the entire world, destroyed my sense of safety; an attack on our homeland was unthinkable but was unfolded right before my eyes. As dawn slowly crawled by darkness I woke to the routine of another day, and staggered into the kitchen still half asleep my body wrapped in an old green terrycloth bathrobe sizes too large, and turned on the television to see if the world was still there like I do every morning. As I grabbed my diet lemon yogurt from the refrigerator, I sat down on the wooden kitchen chair and tucked my feet around the worn rungs to get them off the cold tile floor waiting for the old Wedgwood stove oven to begin to warm the room. I watched San Francisco's Channel 7 news, which was broadcasting a picture of the Twin Towers of the World Trade Center in New York City. There was a live shot and an announcement that a small plane had struck one of the towers at 8:46 EST. That was interesting news and jolted me to the reality of the day. It made sense to me because the Towers were so tall. I had not long ago bought a book on the Towers while browsing around in Costco because I thought they were indeed an engineering marvel. I had read that Tower One was 1709 feet including its antenna, and Tower Two was 1362 feet. The news media blasted out their opinions and more facts that not too many of us knew or really at that time even cared about. I rushed through the house to wake up my husband, Lou, as I heard the announcers tell the television audience that in 1945 an Army Air Force B-25 crashed into the 80th floor of the Empire State Building. It had to be a similar accident. What else could it be? What had really happened was unconscionable. I was barely awake and these facts and thoughts of terrorism were cascading through my brain running stress throughout my entire system. For a fleeting moment I thought I might be dreaming and would wake up and everything would be okay. I was confused and worried. I had not experienced WWII and didn't know the fear people lived through at that time in our history. But, an attack on America was unthinkable. Yet, here it was no warnings, no nothing. This couldn't be happening!

The real story quickly unfolded. Terrorists had used American Airlines Flight 11 Boeing 767 non-stop from Boston to Los Angeles as a missile. It turned south from Albany, New York and headed to lower Manhattan and at 8:45 a.m. EST, crashed into the north tower causing an enormous fire and explosion on impact. At 9:03 a.m. EST, United Airlines Flight 175 slammed into the south tower dissolving any thoughts that the public was harboring of it being an accident. The astonished onlookers were mesmerized as they witnessed many people leap from the inferno to their deaths. No one above the impact had a chance of survival. They made the decision to jump rather than face the alternative, which was the intensity of the fire. I cannot imagine the fear. Later photographs showed people jumping, several couples holding hands, and it made me wonder what kind of hell it was up there to force them to make the choice to leap to their deaths. Unbeknown to the jumpers their bodies falling like bombs killed people below. Video cameras were rolling as some of the residents of the neighborhood filmed the incident. The towers shook and moaned for over an hour but no one was prepared for what was about to happen. At 10:05 a.m. EST, the south tower imploded, and twenty-four minutes later the north tower collapsed, killing thousands, and sending a tsunami of ash, asbestos, cement, plastics, and debris chasing terrified people through the streets of lower Manhattan. Jet fuel poured over and throughout the buildings, wreaking havoc, and stimulating fires, and burning individuals on the ground. The collapse killed 343 members of the New York City Fire Department, and twenty-three police officers who were involved in the courageous rescue attempt. Thousands of innocent lives, civilians, paramedics, and EMT's were lost in and around the towers. The contact was so violent it melted the steel structure of the buildings. Only the skeletal remains of the World Trade Center stood, the giant symbol of America demolished and standing in what looked like a nuclear winter. I had woken up to America's worst nightmare. The situation continued to deteriorate with the news that United Flight 77, another Boeing 757 enroute from Washington D.C., with 58 passengers and six crew members crashed into the Pentagon killing 200 people. The nation reeled in shock, thousands died and evacuations had begun.

More news of another flight down in a field in Shanksville, Pennsylvania; everything seemed unreal. I had to get to the Red Cross office where I had been a volunteer in disaster services for quite some time. I knew we would be contacting our mental health teams first and I would most likely be working on a phone bank. It was imperative that we report into the Chapter office this morning. At 9:15 a.m. EST our national disaster relief staff mobilized for immediate emergency response. I not only worked on our local disaster response team, but also was on a national team. I knew I was going to be activated and sent to New York City. This was sheer madness and surely the beginning of a war. I had no idea who attacked us, and was deeply concerned there would be more. Visibly shaken, I first fed our pig, or he would have broken through the fence and eaten the garden for his breakfast, and then quickly tossed grain to the chickens and a flake of oat hay to the goats. I finished my chores knowing in my heart that this life as I knew it would never be the same. Lou and I went to morning Mass at seven o'clock, and then rushed home to hear more about what was happening. All four aircraft were terrorist-controlled with one mission in mind; to kill, but why? It made no sense.

Being a team leader and active member of the Disaster Team, I spent the day at the Chapter office. It was incredibly busy with the phones constantly ringing with nervous people inquiring about the incident, people who wanted to do something and didn't know what they could do. The public was frightened and reaching out to us for information and a security we couldn't even offer ourselves. The Disaster Director gave me a long printout list with the names of all our mental health

professionals. My job was to phone them and find who would be able
to go to New York City. The first call out of New York was for mental
health workers. I spent most of the day on the phones, finding only
a dozen volunteers. It was difficult for some of them to leave their
office commitments. I made a list and gave it to the Disaster Director.
I was available to go out in either the function of Mass Care, or Family
Services. Our National office would notify us who they needed and
when. This would be my fifth national disaster response. I worked in
the Napa earthquake early this year and responded to Washington state
in the aftermath of an earthquake to assist families, then to a big hotel
fire in San Francisco, and finally to Tropical Storm Allison in Houston,
Texas just months before this attack. So, I was somewhat seasoned but
like everyone else not prepared for this.

All non-military planes in the United States were grounded bringing
air transportation to an abrupt standstill. Only military aircraft were
transporting rescue personnel from various agencies around the country.
The Canadian government had shut down all of their airports. Intense
security put an immediate stranglehold on everything. We were all in
shock and I personally was running on adrenaline.

The nearby City of San Francisco, as all other American cities, was
bracing for another attack. Security was in the red mode as they closed
the Bank of America building and the world famous Pyramid building.
Children went home from school, as families everywhere drew closer
together bracing for the worst. All rescue and relief personnel mobilized,
and no one knew what was going to happen next.

This day was to change my life forever. As I tried to deal with this
realization the nation prayed that God would help us all.

12 September 2001 – Wednesday
Healdsburg, California

One of the four hijacked planes crashed in a Pennsylvania field.
There was talk that perhaps the passengers stood up against the terrorists,
thereby, diverting it from hitting the White House. The fourth plane

rammed into the Pentagon in Washington, D.C. On television we were hearing the personal stories of people involved. Planes were still not flying and everyone was petrified with fear. The bravery of the rescue personnel was incredible as we saw them swarm to the site and heard many had died.

Lou and I went to the local junior college for our early morning Italian language classes, but it was difficult to concentrate. After class, we stopped at the Chapter office on the way home to check our status. Being a member of the National Red Cross team, my name was on their list and I had to wait to be deployed. We jumped in and joined the volunteers working on the fundraiser our Chapter was going to try and produce in a week, which amazed me because an event like that usually would take months. They were making plans for a huge public event, "The World Trade Center Aid Picnic". Everyone in the Chapter had gotten involved in the effort, along with local fire and police personnel.

26 September 2001 - Wednesday
Healdsburg/Santa Rosa, California

It has been difficult waiting for my deployment, and working at the Chapter trying to calm the public down. The tension was thick and everyone was on edge still not knowing what would happen next. After spending almost two weeks working on the phones at the Chapter my assignment changed. I reported in before 8:00 a.m. this morning where I met Carl. He was an "old timer" of a volunteer, and was fun to be with, a lighthearted friend and coworker. He drove the ERV (Emergency Response Vehicle) in Houston, Texas in a Mass Care function right after Tropical Storm Allison just three months earlier. We were partners for a couple of days, struggling through the feeding of the hungry, and driving the ERV in areas that suffered from the storm. He was a dedicated, hardworking volunteer and actually the only German-speaking member of our team.

We went in the ERV with the Americorps girl from our Chapter, Ania, to Alcatal, which was a business in Petaluma to a volunteer fair. The sun of an intensely colorful fall shone on the gloom of everyone we met. My son Louis employed at Alcatal showed me his office and the lab where he worked. He is a telecommunications engineer and also a worker on the Disaster Team. We all worked on the Disaster Team, but not all of us were in the National Red Cross system. That system required a work commitment of weeks, special training, and for some volunteers that was not a feasible arrangement.

At the fair, we set up a table at the back of the emergency vehicle where we gave out health and safety information and pamphlets on disaster preparedness. The parking lot had about twenty various organizations in the county represented. They had information, buttons, free samples, applications, etc. There was an abundance of services accessible to the public, and people wandered around talking to the volunteers at the various tables. I was on edge, waiting for orders to go and concerned about what else was going to happen. As I was unloading some boxes, my cell phone rang and my Disaster Director informed me, I had 24-hours to report to New York City.

We immediately closed down our table and headed back to the office. As we were going up the Old Redwood Highway in Sonoma County, a county truck roared past us over the double line, sideswiping our vehicle and totaling the mirrors. Poor Carl! It was not his fault, but it was the second time the emergency response vehicle had gotten into an accident with him driving. I felt sorry for him. The other driver felt terrible hitting an emergency vehicle and kept apologizing as we exchanged pertinent insurance information. We limped back to the office with no rear view mirrors and a vehicle that would be out of service for at least a week.

When I returned, I picked up my travel check, but had to wait for an interview with the nurse. It was customary to visit with the office nurse before leaving on a national assignment. I also had to wait for the airlines to call me back confirming my flights. This time out, I was to get a round trip ticket. When it had gotten tough in a flood in Houston, some of our workers walked off the job, but with a round-trip ticket taking some effort to change, it might make someone think twice before doing that. The assignment was a hardship job both physically and mentally, so staffing had informed me. It was a no brainier to figure that out. There would be no medical care, and no transportation provided for our teams in New York. I was sure I could handle that. I figured if I lived through the job in Houston, I could do anything. Anyway, I considered it not so much a job, but a privilege. Every American wanted to help in some way, and I could because I was trained and ready to go.

THE AFTERMATH
27 September 2001 – Thursday
Healdsburg, California - New York, New York

I was about to enter the world of the DR (Disaster Response) – 787 New York World Trade Center, the most difficult job of my career as a disaster relief worker.

My husband, Lou, and I left the house in the shadowed darkness of predawn for the nearby City of Santa Rosa to catch the Airport Express bus to SFO (San Francisco International Airport). I was apprehensive and anxious to get to New York as quickly as possible. The Santa Rosa airport was too small for jets to land, but the San Francisco Airporter bus picked up passengers at that location, their last stop in Sonoma County north of San Francisco. Increased security measures prevented us from driving to the bus stop. No unauthorized vehicles could approach the terminal. We parked and dragged my two bags up to the bus area. I would return in approximately one month. My husband, Lou, said goodbye in a subdued manner because he was worried not only about our country, but the job I was about to undertake. It was dangerous and he was concerned about my safety. I was uneasy not knowing if the terrorist would hit California, or what their next move would be. He, being retired military, was tolerant of my leaving on national assignments. He totally understood my motivation for responding to the job. No matter what danger was ahead, I had to go to New York to do my part in combating terrorism and bringing disaster relief to the victims of the incident. The ride to the city was quiet and the bus had few passengers. I arrived at the San Francisco airport at 8:30 a.m. There was a large heavily armed military presence and an incredible amount of security to go through. The personnel at the airport refused my disaster relief worker's identification because they said the date of issue was too old. It was stamped "2000". I also had a current dependent's military identification, an American passport, and a California driver's license, which worked. The security check was tough. The authorities searched everything I had, including me. As a uniformed officer went through my bags, I reached over to catch something that fell from the suitcase and the man snapped, "Don't touch anything." I quickly withdrew my hand. The police were polite, but it was unnerving, and it created tension, although only a whisper of what was to come. I sat in the waiting area and observed in three hours hardly any planes take off, and few passengers past security. The usual busy airport was like a ghost town. Two other disaster workers from my chapter arrived on the scene – Patti and Cymi. I was delighted to see them because I somehow couldn't visualize myself alone at midnight in New York City, a place I had never even visited trying to figure out how to get to the Brooklyn Chapter. We sat and talked and waited. The airport was quiet and the people were dismal, but the bar was doing a good business selling liquid courage. The incoming flights also had very few passengers aboard.

We boarded a Delta 767, with less than a quarter of the seats occupied. I'd never seen anything like it. People were so afraid. I walked down the ramp and dreaded boarding. I stepped onto the plane and my stomach did a flip, as I wondered if we were going to become a missile, or remain a passenger plane. When we were seated, the captain's voice came over the loud speaker telling us we would be safe, and that he wouldn't fly if he thought for a moment we wouldn't be. With a touch of humor he told us he had personally searched the entire aircraft. Believing him, I turned the three seats into one, got a bunch of pillows, and settled in for my flight to Dallas, Texas. On national jobs we seldom had the luxury of nonstop flights to any destination flying the most economical way. Delta flew us free on this disaster, but there was still a transfer to contend with.

We arrived in Dallas safely and deplaned to stretch our legs. I couldn't believe I was back in Texas, but there I was. I had spent a month working with victims of Tropical Storm Allison, and was so glad to leave because the climate was severe, and the job was excruciatingly difficult. There was a terrible accident at the worksite during our disaster response in Texas. It claimed the life of my coworker, and left me feeling vulnerable with an intense awareness of the element of danger in the work I had chosen as a career.

Patty, Cymi, and I took a walk around the boarding area just to get the kinks out. We were quiet and full of anxiety and uncertainty. Our adrenaline was at an all-time high, rushing throughout our bodies assuring us it would be a long time before we would be able to sleep.

Finally, it came time to reboard. We were to stay on the same plane, just pick up more passengers and wait for takeoff. The destination was La Guardia, and the crew gave us a warm welcome, commending our courage. The flight attendants told us if there was anything we wanted, it was to be free. The atmosphere in the plane was tense, but friendly. The passengers were so nervous that they were all conversing with each other, which I had never experienced on a flight before. The tension in that plane seemed to have a life of its own, hanging thick in the air like a heavy fog.

One of the passengers, a businessman about thirty-five years old, who had been working at the World Trade Center at the time of the attack, told us he lost his shoes while trying to escape, and that his feet were still in pain from glass cuts. He had even seen bodies falling from the tower. As he sipped his bourbon from a small flask he removed from his brown jacket pocket, he told us when he passed through security he was pulled aside and taken to a room where he was strip searched. He was a Puerto Rican, wearing clean brand name sports clothing, and with a gentle manner, but he looked like an Arab with his dark skin and black hair. I listened to his story and wondered what I was going to hear in the next month. What was happening to my country? I was heart-broken that the terrorists had had the power to impact us the way they did.

The flight had a few more people, but still wasn't even a quarter full. We flew at 1,000 feet coming out of Dallas-Fort Worth, until we left the populated area. Then our flight began to climb. I had never experienced that before and didn't know why. There was a lot happening I didn't understand. The flight seemed long, but we finally arrived in New York without any problems.

New York at night from the air was like a blanket of jewels. It is a beautiful city, more awesome than Rome. The intensity and spread of the lights both from the buildings and the bridges made San Francisco look like a village. Numerous spotlights illuminated the World Trade Center, a concentration of white light shining through the smoke surrounding the area with a message of death and destruction. It was burning and was a frightening sight. I thought it would be a big piece of Manhattan, but it was only a section of the city, a gaping wound in the colorful landscape, screaming out in pain and agony to the entire world.

28 September 2001 – Friday
New York

When we landed, the crew thanked us over the loud speaker for being in New York. We had slipped into another day as we arrived at the airport. I immediately called home to let Lou know I had arrived without incident. When we got to the luggage claim I phoned headquarters, and was told to go directly to the Park Central, a businessman's hotel situated in Times Square.

When we arrived at ground transport, some of the passengers had gotten there before us, and were busy arranging for a van to the hotel for $85. The three of us looked at each other and said no way. We got a cab for $30 and quickly escaped. After experiencing many high speed rides in cabs around the world, I told the cab driver, I wasn't about to be his passenger if he planned on driving like a madman. He was not only a good driver, he told us in a thick Spanish accent about all the sights we were passing. There were roadblocks, and he drove for quite awhile weaving up and down side streets trying to get us to our destination. The city was a war zone with heavily armed police, and soldiers on every corner, military vehicles and blockades. I saw a man thrown up against his car and the soldiers searching him. I was glad we had negotiated the fare ahead of time. Upon arriving at the hotel we paid the driver. I gave him five additional dollars and thanked him for driving with such care. He cracked a smile through his tired, unshaven face and reciprocated by thanking us for being in New York.

We arrived at our midtown Manhattan hotel before dawn, only to notice dozens of stores open for business. I soon discovered that New York City never sleeps. I checked in and put my luggage in my room, too tired to unpack. However, I did remove my gray and white Red Cross uniform work apron, neatly folded it and put it under my arm and went out to buy a piece of fruit for a snack. After making my small purchase, I then walked back to the hotel lobby to wait for transportation to headquarters. I had a comfortable room on the 18th floor and I was to discover it was quiet. It had been many hours, soon to be a couple of days, since I had slept. I thought a van would pick us up at 6:30 a.m. but a full-sized bus came with more than forty workers, who had come from all over the states. The adrenaline wrapped the workers up in its web, bringing the energy level to a ten. The bus took us out of Manhattan and over the Brooklyn Bridge and to the Brooklyn headquarters. I thought it strange that there were no cars on the bridge, just police and military vehicles, because unknown to me, the bridge was only open to emergency personnel.

Our destination was an old building that sat on the edge of a lovely park at the foot of the Brooklyn Bridge. The incident had caused the building to burst with more staff than it could hold. The Chapter building was headquarters for the operation, and was a madhouse. I got my staffing paper and went through the various offices getting directions and carefully followed them, trying not to fall asleep. I ended up at the Family Service office where I waited for an assignment.

We filled out forms for assignments; a service center in lower Manhattan was Cymi's destination. Even Patti and I couldn't stay together because the man in charge said it wouldn't be possible. I looked at the papers I was filling out and realized how actively involved I was with my home Chapter. I think my experience had a great influence on my assignment. I was assigned to Ground Zero at the World Trade Center while Patti went to White Plains, New York. She was in a service center, whereas I would be working as far as I knew in the Red Zone on a team in damaged apartment buildings assisting the people with their immediate emergency needs. The apartment buildings, like everything in New York, were enormous, housing thousands of people. A Family Service coordinator talked to me at great length, informing me what I was to expect from the job. I was to spend the rest of the day filing in the office. Tomorrow I would join my team. I didn't mind, but I was so tired I could hardly focus on the work. I had been up for more than 30 hours.

Before I could begin my assignment, I had to have my photograph taken for an identification card. The worker in the basement office took my picture and gave me a plastic identification card that said "Full Access to Ground Zero", which I was to wear on a chain around my neck any time I was working. It was white with a green strip running along the bottom. The other workers received white cards with a yellow strip, not allowing them to Ground Zero. I was totally aware it was going to be a difficult mission and that only a small minority of relief workers was in the Red Zone. As I slipped the chain around my neck and looked down at my green card, the clerk in his Red Cross apron and soiled black pants said, "Welcome to Hell". He startled me because I didn't know what to expect, and he sounded like he had already been there. I had the same feeling in the pit of my stomach I had when I boarded the plane in San Francisco, except there was no pilot with his jokes to relax me.

After the clerk gave me my new identification card, he filled me in on some of the rules at the site, one being to pay close attention to the warning system of the air horn: one blast was an alert to danger; two meant to run for your life, and three was an all-clear. There was chatter of another attack and at that point I had to make a choice between leaving or staying to assist the people. I chose to stay.

When I got the ID, I headed for a staff meeting where I was informed that at all times we were to remain strong in front of our clients, and I knew that would probably be easier said than done. I still had only a small idea of what I was getting into. They also informed us we weren't supposed to wear any obvious identification connecting us to our teams on the streets because we would be targets. Target for whom? The staff felt there was a risk to our safety because of the volatility of the situation. "Be careful – be safe" became a slogan on the street, and I heard it over and over again.

In the office on the blackboard, I saw a written notice that thousands of rescue and relief workers from all over the country were in the vicinity of the "pit" which was the name of the area I would be working around. We had respite centers, one of which was a luxury ship, *The Spirit of New York* docked at Pier 11. Everyone involved in the job welcomed the hot meals served aboard. The ship would later move to the boat basin at the site near the Winter Garden, which once was a beautiful glass enclosed building housing stores and a central area with benches and palm trees that seemed to grow out from the polished marble floors, a sweeping marble staircase that led to other office buildings, and an area for public entertainment with a wonderful view of the Hudson River. Behind the Winter Garden and across the highway was the World Trade Center. The Mass Care personnel were working on the ship supporting the overworked police, fire, and rescue personnel with hot meals, a place to rest, free phone calls and adjustments by skilled chiropractors.

"Listen for the air horn. Be safe!" That was the daily warning for all the workers going to Ground Zero. I wore my work clothes which consisted of black jeans, a Red Cross baseball type cap, a team jacket covered by the Red Cross gray and white apron with the large red cross on the back with the words, "American Red Cross Disaster Relief" below the cross, and my identification into the Red Zone because the security was intense and it was required. We had to wear our "uniform" clothing on the metro and the streets because we were going directly into the Red Zone. The Family Service manager also told us about the terror and stress we were going to be working in at the site. She said if any of us felt we would get too emotional, she didn't want us going in. She was nice about not making anyone feel inadequate. It was like the old cliché, "If you can't stand the heat, stay out of the kitchen," but none of us knew how hot that kitchen was going to be. I was confident that I could do the job. I worked out at home to remain physically fit and emotionally I was stable, but I had no idea what I was going to see, smell, and hear in the next month.

Finally, the staff noticed that workers who had arrived in New York at midnight, and had not slept, were no longer functioning at a useful level. Can you imagine the mess of those files with workers that tired? Anyway, they finally told us to leave and report back first thing in the morning after we had gotten some sleep. We had no return transportation to Manhattan, so I decided to take the subway. I had never been to New York or Brooklyn and had not a clue how the trains operated or what train went where. There were two women from Missouri, who were also going to Park Central Hotel, but were afraid of getting lost, but I wasn't concerned, so we went together. I never feared finding my way because, if worse came to worst, there were cabs.

The subway entrance was next door to headquarters, which made it easy. We went down three flights of stairs, leaving the daylight behind to a booth near the boarding platform. A young black woman in uniform with tight corn rolls and brown horn-rimmed glasses was sitting behind a thick Plexiglas window reading a movie magazine which covered her identification card that hung on a faux pearl chain around her neck. I had to shout to penetrate her glass prison, just so I could purchase a Metro card. I could only speak to her on a microphone, and even at that she could hardly hear me. She rattled off the different Metro cards for sale, and their prices. I plunked out $17 and bought a card good for a week on the trains, or the local busses. The other two women used coins to slip past the turnstile, whereas I just zipped my card through a slot above the turnstile and entered quite smoothly. Later I discovered we could have ridden free because of our disaster relief work, but the clerk never bothered to mention that fact to me.

There was a diverse mixture of people on the train, their different languages blending into melodic, harmonious sounds and in a strange sort of way comforting me. It was about a ten minute ride for us to reach 59th Street. When we stepped off the train, the two women went in different directions, and were immediately lost in the crowd. A train roared by almost taking my team cap with its draft wind, and I was alone. I went up the stairs to a different level, still in the subway, and then wasn't sure where to go. I saw four police officers talking and I approached them. Against the advice from the office, I was wearing my team jacket with its obvious Red Cross logo on the back. I hadn't brought any other jacket with me to New York, so I had little choice because I was cold. I was carrying my work vest under my arm, along with copies of my staffing papers. They cordially greeted me, and one officer volunteered to walk me to the hotel. He was a tall, young, dark haired Italian-American, who it turned out, was married and lived in Queens. He stopped after we had walked for a couple of blocks, and showed me some school pictures of his four kids. He said he was pleased our teams had come to help, and if there was anything I ever needed just to stop an officer, and he or she would assist me. He warned me to stay out of the subways. He had strong feelings about an impending chemical attack and according to him it was going to take place in the underground. He said it would be a gas attack and to be careful of myself. At that point, I became keenly aware that I was going to have to be more attentive of my surroundings. The officer was good company, walking the six blocks down busy streets to my hotel. Pedestrians smiled at us as we passed.

I had learned from traveling that when I landed in a new location never to go to bed until it was night. I was so tired, when I arrived back at the hotel, but I wanted to adapt as quickly as possible to the new time zone, so I went out to shop for a coat. I had not brought warm enough clothing and after walking a few blocks near the hotel found a small department store with a sale on coats. I purchased a black goose down quilted three-quarter length jacket. I walked around observing the people and enjoying the cold air and the warmth of the new coat. The people in Manhattan were so interesting. They were dressed in fashionable clothing, mostly black, and the women had interesting, chic, often short haircuts and they always seemed to be in a hurry. The New Yorkers were friendly and were responsive if spoken to, shattering their reputation for being cold and uncaring. Maybe the hit on the towers made them more aware of how important we all were. Not able to stay awake a minute more, I returned to the hotel and fell asleep at dusk.

29 September – Saturday
Manhattan, New York

I went downstairs to the hotel lobby to catch the 6:30 a.m. bus to headquarters. The bus was full and bustling with energy, adrenaline pumping through the crowd of excited volunteers, who had hopes of making a difference in someone's life, or maybe out just for the adventure. I couldn't find anything to laugh and joke about considering what had occurred. Just driving through Manhattan was like someone driving a stake through my heart. The evidence of war surrounded us: streets guarded by army personnel stopping and searching vehicles, blockades, heavily armed police, many with dogs, and heavy, thick air filled with a film of smoke and stink. Nothing was normal and wouldn't be for a long, long time. The volunteers were behaving more like a group of people on a tour bus. I wondered when the reality of the great tragedy would hit them.

When we arrived at headquarters in Brooklyn, we had to go through a security checkpoint before we could enter the three-story building. Two large black men bundled up in navy blue security uniforms, mufflers, and stovepipe knit caps searched through my bag, checked my identification card, smiled and handed me a copy of the <u>New York Times</u> as they waved me on. Once inside, I went upstairs to a Family Services staff meeting in a hot and stuffy room that overlooked the park across from the office. The trees were naked and seemed to bend in the wind, peeking in the windows at our meeting. The weather had turned nasty with freezing high winds. I received my assignment to an outreach team, when the manager announced to the group of fifty workers he needed someone who wasn't afraid to go out on the streets in the Red Zone to tell people we were there to assist them. I leapt at the opportunity, and was placed on a different team. There were nine of us: Henry, the supervisor, a middle-aged man flown in from Indiana, Louis the mental health worker, an intense older Italian with gentle brown eyes, Joan the retired nurse who came from Arizona and seemed tired all the time, and six disaster relief caseworkers, myself included.

The team left the Chapter right after the meeting, went around the corner and entered the subway down flights of dirty stairs. As we descended into the subterranean world, we could feel the heat and smell the fetid odor from the homeless people sleeping on the wooden benches that lined the tiled walls. We couldn't get to Ground Zero by train because when the Towers fell, the weight collapsed the subways causing the underground transportation to be diverted, not to mention the fact that security was so tight it would have been impossible anyway. After a short ride, we surfaced on smoke-filled streets and walked several blocks to a scene that looked like a Hollywood set. It was surreal to me. We were about to enter a war zone, the entire area south of Canal Street, which was a large piece of Manhattan. It was so different than on television. TV just didn't catch the enormity of the scene. There were chain link fences to keep the media and unauthorized individuals out of the Red Zone that went on for blocks. We climbed stairs and crossed the street through a covered bridge near the 300 block of Chambers Street, from which I saw a large part of the military mobilization. It looked like an entire army with all of their equipment. There was a large blue tent which was housing a temporary morgue. We went downstairs on the other side of the overpass bridge, and waited in a short line by a chain-link fence to show our identification to armed soldiers dressed in camouflage fatigues; they smiled and told us to go ahead. I had passed through the checkpoint. The mountain of rubble was still burning, and it had a smell I was to live with for a month, and never forget for a lifetime. Every agency imaginable was there: Secret Service, FBI, military, police, fire personnel, federal marshals, rescue workers, ironworkers, the Salvation Army, the Red Cross and various members of the clergy.

We walked several blocks to a large gray colored apartment building on a windy corner overlooking the Hudson River. There was no ordinary boat traffic. Armed coast guard cutters waited and watched, anticipating another attack. The streets were void of regular traffic and the residents had all but disappeared.

There were two restricted Zones south of Canal Street, the Yellow Zone and the Red Zone, which both required identification to enter.

The security was tighter around the Red Zone because it was the location of the "pile". The Yellow Zone was any location south of Canal Street, which included dozens of high-rise apartment buildings and businesses. My identification card gave me the freedom to work in both zones. The streets ceased to be a neighborhood, having little evidence of anything civilian on them. There was a strong military presence; police, and emergency telephone stations where people could call anyone, anywhere free. EPA (Environmental Protection Agency) employees and equipment, fire trucks, and a few people, who had shown any identification they had to try to get into the Red Zone to their apartments. The residents were using phone bills, driver's licenses, anything that documented their current addresses. The soldiers and Marines detained many of them, not allowing everyone to pass.

We operated out of a lobby in a huge apartment building. The apartment had a front desk and I kept thinking it was a hotel, but not so. It was interesting because some of the apartment building personnel were working at the front desk despite the danger in the air. Why they were still working was a mystery to me. I think the management was living under the illusion that everything needed to look as normal as possible. The staff of the building was very cooperative in lending us any equipment we needed. They would often talk to us and ask us questions about where we came from and what exactly our job in the area was. I think they would have done anything for us.

We created an instant makeshift office, with three large collapsible tables, and folding chairs, which we placed in front of floor-to-ceiling windows that overlooked the Hudson River. After we set up, I looked out the windows at the neighborhood. Before the attack it was a desirable area with newer, modern, expensive apartments where many families resided. There was a lovely park that ran along the Hudson River shoreline like a long green snake connecting the apartments to the places of business. Many of the residents in the community worked nearby at the World Trade Center, and surrounding buildings. Right in that neighborhood ten towers had been totally destroyed, and later down the line more buildings would be demolished because they were structurally unsound. Gray ash covered buildings next to where the towers once stood with broken windows and large parts of their facades hanging down like torn steel flesh revealing massive mortal wounds. The workers had attached to the side of one building a gigantic American flag that was tattered and torn from the constant wind, a battle flag.

Henry, the supervisor, came over to the window, and told me to go out and find clients. It was so cold and the wind was howling as I stood in front of the building waiting for people to pass. My coat developed a thin layer of ash changing the color from black to gray. There were two police officers sitting in a glass booth nearby attempting to keep out of the wind. I wanted to join them to get warm, but it wasn't possible because I had to locate clients. There weren't many people on the streets because it was so difficult to get into the neighborhood. The people I managed to stop were residents attempting to return to their apartments to investigate the damage and claim their belongings. Being civilians, they weren't allowed vehicles. They could only take what they could carry. No one wanted to stay, because it was doubtful what carcinogenic particles were present in the air. I saw sophisticated gas masks on the faces of many of the people who entered the area. I stopped about fifteen people over the period of an hour, explaining how we were there to assist them with their emergency needs. They were receptive and definitely had needs, but were in a hurry to leave the Red Zone as quickly as possible most faces reflecting sheer panic. I spoke with people, many of whom couldn't even put a sentence together correctly. They were scared.

I met a young, well-dressed woman on the street who told me about a tenant's meeting taking place as we spoke. I went inside and told Henry that I thought I should go to that meeting to speak to the victims. He was hesitant, but encouraged me. How else were we going to reach the people?

I went into the lobby of an upscale apartment building three blocks further into the Red Zone to the shouts of a large, angry crowd of about one hundred tenants all jammed into a space never meant for that many people. I worked my way to the front of the crowd and announced who I was, and whom I represented. A quiet fell over the room, and suddenly one hundred pairs of eyes were riveted on me as I stood on top of a desk so that everyone could see me. I told them that we were in the area to assist with emergency needs by giving a grant to every person who lived in the neighborhood, and we would also assist them in many more ways, such as emotional care, groceries, rent, and referrals and after interviewing them probably much more. They listened intently as I told them our location and invited them to come and see us. When I finished, I thanked them for their attention and began to work my way to the door. I felt swallowed up by the crowd as I said over and over again, "Excuse me, excuse me, excuse me", and continued to push my way toward the exit. As I let the door slowly close behind me I heard them shouting and saw them shaking their fists at the next speaker who happened to be the landlord. The tension in the lobby was explosive.

I reported back to my supervisor, Henry, informing him of what had transpired at the meeting. He was interested and hoped the tenants would come in for assistance. He told me to go back to work on the street. People from the tenants' meeting almost immediately began to arrive, until our temporary office was so crowded Henry called me back into the building to start doing casework with the families, and writing disbursing orders. (We called them DO's. They were forms we used to disburse money and goods to the clients.) I was glad because my hands were blue from the cold and I thought my nose might just drop off. They were anxious to tell their stories, and all day I heard tales of terror and death, one after another.

A young woman sat in front of me holding her husband's hand as he cried and told me his story. It wasn't the loss of his job or apartment that was tearing him apart. When the attack occurred he was in his office with his secretary, a young single-mother of two from the Bronx. She stood by the window after the explosion and watched the golden shards of glass rain down to the street below, the sun's reflection changing them from yellow to gold, and strange shades of green. Mesmerized like a horse by fire, she died. He had begged her to run for the stairs, but unable to move, she chose to die in the rain of fire. He escaped down 59 flights of stairs to the lobby and the street below. Her image was imbedded in his head and bored deep into my brain. He kept saying, "I should have just dragged her out of there, but I was so afraid I ran." His wife was crying and I was groping for the correct words to keep them from falling apart. As I opened a case for them I gave the mental health worker a high sign, and when the client finished speaking to me, Louis, our mental health worker, came over and started speaking to him. They moved to a quiet corner and I took another client.

After many more heartbreaking stories, I told Henry I was going to lunch. He suggested I go to the ship docked across from the World Trade Center at the North Cove Marina often called the Boat Basin. The *Spirit of New York* had recently moved there for the rescue and relief personnel.

"*The Spirit of New York* became involved in the disaster response when Captain Greg Hanchrow of Spirit Cruises of New York was looking for ways that Spirit Cruises could assist in the relief effort. The normal docking locations of the Spirit Cruises are at Chelsea Piers in Manhattan and in Weehawken, N.J. In order to create respite services at the Trade Center site they temporarily relocated their *Spirit of New York* vessel to North Cove. Most of the crew consisted of volunteers from Spirit Cruises ranks and from the outside community. There were about 20 captains, mates, deckhands, and managers on the payroll. On September 14, at the urging of Captain Hanchrow, the *Spirit of New York* went into service as a floating respite center. This undertaking was in conjunction with restaurateurs Daniel Boulud, Gary Kunz and Don Pintabona (then the Executive Chef of Tribeca Grill) for a program later named the "*Chefs with Spirit*" initiative. Approximately 25,000 shifts were filled in a four week period. Plenty of volunteers were available. They served an estimated 8,000 meals each day.

On board the *Spirit of New York*, food was available 24-hours a day to feed the rescue and recovery workers, law enforcement officials, and volunteers from across the country. A ship was an ideal respite service solution for many reasons. Whereas the majority of downtown Manhattan was initially filled with debris, cruise ships, such as the *Spirit* were allowed unfettered access to downtown via the waterways. Also, for the first several days, there was no electricity nor was there plumbing to the downtown area. The boat provided a floating, self-contained "clean" environment for the relief workers who had no where else to go." [1]

I walked with Clare, a worker from my team. She was a young Irish woman from New York with red hair and freckles making her look even younger than she was. She was very dedicated to the work we were doing, but extremely nervous and always seemed to be looking for something often gazing past me while we talked. We strolled along what once was a lovely tree-lined walkway for about six blocks, and headed for a hot lunch aboard the *Spirit of New York*. I had never been so cold. We zigzagged through construction, barricades, memorials of flowers and teddy bears, rescue personnel and a fleet of military, police, and fire vehicles. We stood and watched the rescue dogs prowling through the rubble searching for human remains. The stress was so intense, it took over the bodies and minds of the workers, reflecting out through glazed-over eyes, and dirty tired faces.

My first impression of the "pile" was a mountain of dust, concrete, and steel. I smelled death; it permeated my clothing sinking into my soul, as I breathed the pulverized bones of the dead. There were I-beams twisted and folded like giant pickup sticks. The rubble was eight stories high and the rescue teams were still digging hoping to find human life, bodies, or body parts. It was burning and the smoke covered me with a cocoon of fear and tied me up with the strings of its stress. The smoke continually rose from the guts of this hell. There was a somber air about the entire area, and a strange quiet among the workers. There were bits of paper everywhere and residue from all of the destroyed offices. The workers at the site looked exhausted with haunting stares giving their faces the looks of old men and women. As I stood there I wondered what street I was on. There was no way to identify any names of the streets. Would I be able to find them if I ever returned here? How would I know where I worked? Strange questions rattled around my brain.

As the search went on, there were more body parts than complete cadavers found. Carried to the morgue in white buckets were various parts of human remains. The attack had left devastation like nothing

I had ever seen, or ever hoped to see again. I was overwhelmed and almost unable to grasp the reality of the scene.

We continued to walk, and right before we got to the ship, Clare and I met a woman who had on filthy blue coveralls, a jacket so grimy that I couldn't tell what the color was, black laced-up boots covered with ash, a yellow hard hat, and around her neck hung a respirator. I didn't realize she was a woman until she spoke. She talked to us about how much she appreciated the kindness shown her and how important to her the warm meals were, and the willingness of our people just to take the time to listen to her when she couldn't handle the stress any longer. She had two dogs standing next to her with donated booties on their sore paws. The mud encrusted dogs were working as rescue/cadaver dogs on the hot burning pile. Most of the dogs working the "pile" didn't have booties on because they needed to splay their feet to keep their balance but the public had made the booties to hopefully protect the animals. Many of the dogs had already died on the "pile". One dog was a short-haired black and white border collie mix and the other a black lab mix, not the stereotypical animals seen on television doing rescue work. The dogs appeared to be exhausted with their heads hanging down and the woman had a dreadful sadness in her dark brown eyes. As we said goodbye we told her we appreciated her comments and we continued our walk toward the ship.

There were about twenty small pleasure boats docked in the boat basin along the way. Gray ash and unidentifiable debris covered them, giving them the appearance of ghost ships, rocking back and forth on the water, all mourning the death and destruction that surrounded them. Docked at the end of the pier was *The Spirit of New York*.

We boarded the ship and entered the lower deck. Red Cross Mass Care was serving a buffet with a variety of hot food donated by local restaurants. It was wonderful, tasted good, and had a comforting affect on everyone. There were rows of tables both circular and rectangular and about one hundred people were eating lunch. On the tables there were token wreaths and cards from school children thanking everyone for their hard work. The workers looked so weary, and the mood was solemn. Normally walking into a large public eating area I would hear laughter and the drone of conversation. It was quiet. We ate a hardy meal of roast beef and potatoes.

"The ship had electricity and running water. It was self-contained and included generators, portable water tanks, and sewage systems. Local restaurants augmented the provisions and staffing that Spirit Cruises was able to provide. One of the most vivid memories of the days following the tragedy according to David Sinclair, General Manager of Spirit Cruises was of famous chef Bobby Flay cooking Raman Noodles to make sure that rescue workers were fed." [2]

I was amazed at this boat and later contacted the company to just give them a little feedback on what comfort we found there while working under such terrible circumstances.

They told me that: "The *Spirit of New York* provided crucial assistance immediately following the 9/11 tragedy. The *Spirit of New York* vessel is roughly 185 feet in length with a 35 foot beam. The interior cabins of the vessel include three dining decks, a full galley and other amenities such as rest rooms and cold storage.

The boat had food and beverages available on deck two and the stern of deck one. The chairs and tables were removed from the third deck so that sleeping bags could be laid out to create a 'quiet zone' where workers, many of whom were working around the clock, could rest for a few hours. The bow of deck one was used to store donations as well as to distribute the non-food donations such as clean underwear, socks, gloves, and masks. Over time, more services were added to the respite center. Once phone service was restored, AT&T provided a bank of telephones with free long distance so that workers could contact their families. Massage therapists from local day spas provided back rubs to help relieve some of the aches caused by heavy lifting. Entertainers and political figures used the space and the break time to chat with workers in order to keep morale up."[3]

We left, walking back in the freezing wind to our workplace. The meal had warmed me up somewhat and had at least re-energized me. The wind twisted my nametag chain around my neck in a tight knot. The police and military always looked for our identification and, if they didn't see it, would stop us. I had my work vest on and under that my new coat, just trying to stay warm. The air was full of pollutants and my eyes burned and watered. Near the Winter Garden a fireman saw me rubbing them and he stopped to give me eye drops - bottled tears which I appreciated. I had a mask on my arm, but didn't use it because it steamed up my sunglasses and I couldn't see where I was going. It was so thin that it would immediately get coated inside with gray ash and gag me when I did wear it. I wondered why we weren't issued safety masks. The masks that I got from Red Cross were totally inappropriate. The EPA kept telling us it was safe, so I didn't think it mattered, but the air was thick and smelled like death.

As we walked back to our apartment office, I reflected on the site itself and just generally on the atrocity. The destructive influence of the attack spread throughout the entire neighborhood, leaving it void of its usual life. The thick dust covered the remaining buildings, which gave the illusion they had all been painted the same drab gray color. The well-manicured playgrounds became helicopter pads. It was as if children had never lived there. It made me angry that the terrorists had created such wanton damage leaving innocent people devastated and disrupting lives for God knows how long. The scenes at Ground Zero were a challenge to anyone who wanted to describe them in any detail. They were almost beyond description.

When I returned, I did casework for the rest of the day because I had brought so many people in. I worked alone without a partner, with my papers piled on a brown folding table in the lobby of the apartment building, with the view of the river and the ravaged neighborhood. The interviews were sad. It broke my heart to hear about the children that saw the planes hit the buildings, and the stories of fear and terror of families trying to get their lives back together. I had given myself to the service of humanitarian relief work, and I was mentally paying the price of compassion. Every story stuck in my soul and worked on my mind. I totally related to the pain of my clients, but had to remain strong in front of them. It was an arduous assignment, but I was still grateful that I had the training to do it.

As it grew dark, we closed our makeshift office. We had done forty-five cases, which was phenomenal. We walked back to the subway through security checkpoints and past cyclone fences where the army and police stood guard. When we got outside of the Red Zone, there were crowds of people trying to get pictures and watching in strained silence. People smiled at us as we passed. They said, "God Bless You." A woman handed me a flier that stated all the personnel working in the Red Zone could get free haircuts at her shop in Tribeca. Everyone was trying to help in any way they could.

Tribeca was an interesting neighborhood with old red brick buildings that looked like they were once factories. Actually, it was a neighborhood undergoing birth pains among the smoke of death. It was one of the city's choicest residential districts. Rents were almost beyond reach for renovated warehouses and lofts abandoned years ago, but now attracting artists, young business professionals, small businesses, and families. As we left, I looked back before we entered the underground and saw the smoke rising from the destruction; it still didn't seem real to me. My mind clicked like an overactive camera stamping images that I would forever carry with me.

After a crowded subway ride, our team arrived at the Chapter in Brooklyn, dirty and tired. We were weary as we checked in through security, and stood patiently as the guards probed our backpacks and briefcases. As we waited, I noticed an announcement taped to the glass door entrance. Mass was being said in the training room, and it had just begun. Two members of my team wanted to attend and we knew we were late. We raced up three flights of stairs, taking them two at a time, ran down a long hall crowded with boxes and emergency supplies, and quietly entered the room where Mass was being said. We tried to slide into the room unnoticed, sitting in the back on cold, gray folding chairs so as to not disrupt the service that had already begun. At the front of the room there was a standard rectangular folding table like the one we had worked on in the apartment lobby, with some yellow daisies in a green vase sitting on the corner. A heavy-set Irish priest who had fat red cheeks, and was dressed in khaki pants, and a blue button-down shirt with a small white stole around his neck was saying Mass in the well-lit room. About sixteen people were in attendance. It was bare bones, but it was comforting. The priest said he wanted everyone to go to communion. He didn't have the water to mix with the sacramental wine, so he used the tap water from the sink behind him. I found the opportunity to stop and pray a great source of strength. Outreach workers were always on the run, and seldom got to enjoy the privileges of the officer workers, who had a regular schedule. So, we took what we could when we could. We were so dirty and smelled of death. The other workers gave us strange looks, but the priest smiled in a special way because he knew by our appearance where we had been working.

After Mass we went to the Records and Reports office to turn in our paperwork and waited in a very long line for what seemed like forever. I left the building and wearily climbed aboard our bus to return to the hotel. I was so tired I fell asleep and was awakened looking into the face of our overweight sweating older bus driver as he said in his unique Brooklyn accent, "Hey lady, didn't they get you a room? You can't sleep on the bus." He smiled and stepped aside for me to leave. I didn't eat dinner but just took the elevator up to my room and went and flopped on my bed fully clothed. It had been a very long day.

30 September – Sunday
Manhattan, New York

The relief workers gathered in small clusters in front of the hotel waiting for the 6:30 a.m. arrival of the bus. The weather was cold and windy; it was dark when we left the hotel and dark when we returned at night. The people on the bus were from every state in the union, as well as the territories of Puerto Rico, and Guam. They were interesting and it was entertaining to listen to their different attitudes and stories.

Army personnel stopped the bus at the many checkpoints and rerouted us several times. The workers were scared and nervous, but tried to disguise it with their jokes and gallows humor. The soldiers were present everywhere, and it gave the appearance of an invasion. The increased security didn't make me feel safe, only uncomfortable. It gave me a sick feeling in the pit of my stomach to know our freedom was threatened to the point that men, and women were standing on our street corners in their camouflage uniforms armed, and ready to do whatever was necessary to protect the city. But, it also took away from us, our freedom of movement.

When we got to the headquarters, I had time to grab a bagel before the staff meeting. I was hungry considering I had skipped dinner the previous night. Henry approached me and asked if it would be possible for me to extend my time in New York. He said I was talented at handling people and knew the paperwork, and to please consider it. I thought I probably would because I knew there were more people I could help, but I was also aware of the fact that the job was taking a toll on my mind and body.

After the meeting, we went down into the subway to catch our ride to the Red Zone. The Metro system was excellent and we never had to wait very long for a train. When we boarded as a team, people would stare at us and often make remarks that were usually positive, but there were the negative ones too. The general population was angry and hadn't even begun to deal with the emotional impact of the attack. I felt like a member of an occupying army, and in a way I was. We would stand on the crowded subway and people sitting would stare at my identification. They would read it and look at me with such empathy and their eyes reflected their sorrow and pain. It was bad enough that the military and police were everywhere but then there we were with badges sticking in people's faces, reminding them even more of where we were going. They knew what we were going to face each day and they were not only angry, but scared. The job was not a response to a natural disaster; we were working in a crime scene and access was restricted. No media was allowed anywhere in the Red Zone, but as I saw later, they were lined up outside the barricades with incredibly powerful cameras hoping for a spectacular picture. Various obstacles like cranes, and other heavy equipment, blinded their cameras' large intrusive eyes. Leaving at night we learned to avoid them. The media was looking to talk to anyone coming out of the area.

My job for the day was to begin by working on the street between two apartment buildings in the Red Zone. I dreaded the cold, but looked forward to finding the people who needed assistance. There was a high wind coming off the Hudson River, and it was absolutely freezing. There were hardly any people around. New Yorkers didn't seem to be early risers, but they did stay out late at night. If they weren't going to work they would most likely be sleeping. I kept ducking into doorways and standing against walls because I just couldn't keep warm. I had developed a bad cough and wasn't sure if it was from the rotten air, or a virus. The cough labeled, "The World Trade Center Cough", later known as the "World Trade Center Syndrome" became a chronic problem for me.

I was able to stop about eight people and direct them to where we set up our makeshift office. I decided to take an early lunch mainly because I wanted to go somewhere warm. I asked my teammate, Ruth, to go with me. She was a young, exceptionally intelligent woman from Israel, with sandy hair and piercing green eyes, a bit taller than I, and could have been a model. As we walked, she told me of her experience with war in Israel. She had been in the army there for two years, and said she understood what the people at Ground Zero were going through. We walked on the promenade along the waterfront past the empty playgrounds and an artificial lake where a police officer was sharing his lunch with the ducks. Several Mallard ducks gathered for a free meal, diving for bread beneath the scum that coated the water and clung to their wings like a thin ice. The rescue workers were digging and cranes were moving giant pieces of concrete. We could smell the dead, which was a constant reminder of the emotional pain we were all feeling.

We boarded *The Spirit of New York* where many were already eating a hot lunch of sausages and beans. We ate with haste because it started getting crowded and the workers needed a place to sit.

After lunch, I went upstairs to the third deck and had a chiropractor adjust my stiff neck and shoulders, which was a great idea. The chiropractor was a man from California. He had volunteered his time and skills to work on the ship hoping to be of assistance to the rescue personnel. The man had the strongest hands and worked rapidly on my sore neck and shoulders. He told me everyone was just too tight from the stress and hard physical work required in digging and moving tons of debris. I couldn't disagree. On the same deck of the ship there were mattresses lined up next to each other on the floor near the walls. Men were attempting to get some rest before they had to return to hunt for the missing. They slept fully clothed, some with their muddy boots on. A fully dressed man with his German shepherd rescue dog nestled next to him was sound asleep.

On our way back to work we saw a retaining wall that made the grass level instead of slopping downward. The ground in front of the wall was a monument of roses, daisies, carnations all varied in color still in their plastic wraps from the florist shops, and dirty weather-beaten teddy bears were propped along the wall's ledge. It was just a matter of feet from the debris. Taped on the wall were photos of the missing with questions as to their whereabouts. "Have you seen my husband, John?" "Have you seen my daughter? Please call." "Samantha is Missing – Age 24." "Missing Heroes" (a photo showing eight New York firefighters) "My husband Harry worked at Regus Tower 2 – 93rd Floor. If you have any information, please call." Neatly produced on computers with scanned in photographs, the fliers from the families of the missing screamed out in desperation for help; there were fliers written in nervous scrawls of frantic family members, and glued on photos. Someone had actually just written on the wall describing a missing person with no photo, but with the usual cry to help find his or her loved one. There was a flier showing a black man with his family at a birthday party standing by him. Someone had drawn a big red circle around his face indicating he was missing. Below the picture was scribbled a telephone number. There were dozens and dozens of pictures of missing firemen. We stood there quietly for a moment to whisper a silent prayer, show our respect, and choke back our tears.

When we returned, I started doing casework. I did about eight cases in the afternoon into the early evening hours interviewing each client with the utmost empathy. The tenants had difficulty telling me their stories without crying. Trying to process their losses left them traumatized and most were still in shock. Many had to leave their pets behind, which was a major issue causing some of them to sneak back in through the military barricades, just to rescue them. They no doubt considered the pets family members. I saw soldiers talk to people who were from the neighborhood and wave them through the barricades when told about how important it was for them to retrieve their abandoned pets.

We were working at Ground Zero and had moved closer into another apartment lobby in South End, an area with some of the worst damage. Tenants were gathering personal effects in their apartments, but only what they could carry because they had to walk in and then back out of the Red Zone, which was quite a distance. For small increments of time the tenants collected their most valued possessions and then left for a safe haven somewhere else in Manhattan, and in some cases even outside the city.

There was a thick layer of some sort of dust all over the lobby, which made it difficult to breathe. As I interviewed tenants, others were leaving in droves. They were taking out bags and baggage, deserting their furniture, and many of their personal belongings. They wanted to get out of the neighborhood even if it cost them a lawsuit regarding broken leases. They were terrified. They asked me if I wanted their clothing, or the personal possessions they were leaving behind. I had no suggestions for them. They couldn't even donate what remained in their apartments because no civilian trucks could get into the Red Zone. They were not thinking clearly and functioning under the influence of sheer panic. It was difficult for all of them, and it was painful for us to watch.

I continued to work through the afternoon when my supervisor came to me and complimented my case file work. He liked the way I wrote my narratives. He said they were analytical and to the point. Being articulate was vital because for every client I was building a case, so they would receive the utmost in benefits. My words on the paper were important and were the only information another caseworker would have when in the future he or she would pick up the file. They had to be thorough and clearly written.

At the end of a lengthy day, we left in the pouring rain for the subway. It was a long walk and in the middle of the restricted area Henry got into an argument with a tall, stubborn soldier because he wouldn't let us pass a certain street we had full access to. We finally, thank God, went the other way. Everyone was on edge; the stress was like an angry demon possessing us, making all our jobs more complicated. Everyone was exhausted but kept working, one more body, or part to be found, one more client to help. There was no end to it.

When I got to headquarters, I decided I wouldn't wait for the bus. Margaret, a large, big-boned, older woman from headquarters, asked me to go to the hotel on the subway with her, and I thought okay; it would be faster. She was an odd person and there was just something about her that made me uncomfortable. Perhaps it was her lack of grooming and her flighty attitude, but who was I to judge. So, off we went, which was a big mistake!

First, I must tell you the New York subways were an underground world that never ended. We got off at 42nd Street, which was Times Square, and she wanted to transfer to another train that was supposedly closer to the hotel. We marched underground for what seemed like a mile to my tired feet through the grimy tunnels with the tiled walls plastered with advertisements and dirt, passing vendor stands that sold magazines, candy, and cigarettes, and a violinist playing light classical music with his violin case open hoping for the commuters to throw in a coin or two as the ribbons of the sounds of Strauss slithered through the crowds. The subway was a world of its own. It seemed to be as jam-packed with people as the streets above. She admitted she must have taken the wrong turn. Let me interject here that Margaret had a desk job, and my body was so tired that it was hardly functioning. She then went down a flight of stairs, which found us at a platform full of weird characters. I said, "Margaret, I am tired. I'm out of here. I'm taking the train to 59th Street." She agreed, so we went back to the Times Square platform. We were deep into the subterranean world, and along came a police officer shouting, "Clear out! This is closed. Clear out QUICKLY." I said I was going up on the street. I was too tired both from work, and of her, to deal with a bomb scare. She and everyone else followed like rats leaving a sinking ship; all of us had become hyper vigilant. It was like watch your back every waking moment. We surfaced on 42nd Street, leaving us with ten blocks to walk. That was okay, until she started making remarks about me being afraid of everything. I said,

"Hey lady, it's not fear; it's common sense." I started to think: Wait a minute, Patch what are you doing here taking abuse and following this goofy lady? As she began quickly to walk ahead of me and continued her lecture, I hailed a cab, jumped in, gave the cabbie the hotel name and was home in five minutes. As we drove by her, I noticed she was continuing her lecture without me. That lightened up my day a bit.

At the hotel I got into the elevator where a curious older couple asked me if there was a convention in the city. They had spotted my work vest and my identification, which I wore most of the time. I had a slight odor of the dead that clung to my clothing, and ash all over my shoes and dirt on my face. I found it hard to believe that they would think I was at a convention. I told them we were working at the disaster site. They were shocked. What did people think that a huge event like that would disappear in a couple of weeks? Next time, I thought, I'd just take the bus and get in late. At least I wouldn't have to deal with people after work. I was too tired.

In my room I took off my identification card, my work clothes and washed up. I left for a small restaurant around the corner from the hotel. I was so tired I didn't even get the name of the place. I had a big bowl of warm stew. I liked the restaurant because it was quiet, the food was excellent, and I could sit and write without being bothered.

1 October - Monday
Manhattan, New York

I left the hotel at 4:45 a.m. to buy a muffin across the street, and some stamps at the nearby deli. I entered the store and told the small man behind the counter I wished to purchase some stamps for postcards. He opened an old cigar box that contained first class stamps. Not being able to get stamps anywhere, I opted to take the thirty-four cent ones. He smiled with yellow teeth protruding from his thin-lipped mouth and said in broken English, "Fifty-seven cents each". I left with no stamps. Then I crossed the street and bought a blueberry muffin, which turned out to be a stale chocolate chip muffin. I returned it wondering what the rest of the day was going to be like.

The bus to headquarters was on time. Some of the people I had worked with in Houston had arrived. Robin, the radio operator, and I chatted for a while. I was happy to see a friend. Sometimes my jobs got lonely. Actually, a national relief worker lived a lonely lifestyle. We were late getting to headquarters because of all the roadblocks. When we arrived, we had to go through the usual security check before we could enter the building. I grabbed some bottled water from the cafeteria, signed out my disbursing orders at Records and Reports, picked up my blank case forms from Family Services, and went to a staff meeting. After the meeting we gathered our team outside the front door for a quick briefing, and then headed for the subway to Ground Zero. We took the train to Canal Street, which was as close to work as we could get. We walked single file to the secured Zone where the military checked our identification card and allowed us to pass through the checkpoints. It was a long, cold walk to the apartment building lobby, site of our temporary office. The streets were crowded with emergency vehicles, and there were police and soldiers always in sight. The military personnel were heavily armed, and there were armored Humvees on every block.

Four hours a day was the time allotment for the residents to return to their apartments to remove possessions, and bring in insurance adjusters. There were few civilians on the streets, but I stopped whomever I could to inform them of our services. I told them about our assistance and the benefits we were able to help them with. The people were receptive and many went into the lobby to see our caseworkers.

This morning was an emotional drain. The event was beginning to become real to our clients, and their surreal feelings were waning. In the beginning, because of the magnitude of the attack, it took on the scope of a Hollywood set; no one could grasp the shock of what had happened, so it slipped into a surrealist world all of its own. It was evident that our teams were going to need more mental health workers, and soon.

The cold winds blew between the giant buildings. I got so chilled my nose was red and my fingers were numb. When I went into the lobby to get warm, Henry saw I was shivering, so he told me to stay and do some casework.

I sat at a long portable table, when a grumpy older man in a brown wrinkled sport's suit sat down in front of me. He was livid because he had a top floor apartment and the police in his words had destroyed it. As I let him talk to calm him down, he told me that the authorities had ruined his garden because they were looking for body parts, and had broken his expensive flowerpots and a lovely miniature Carrara marble statue. It was obvious that the man was in shock and that it was controlling his behavior. He told me that in the process of the search, the officers had discovered two arms tied together at the wrists. I was so overwhelmed that whatever he said after that I don't think I heard.

When I finished his case, I told Henry I was going to go back on the streets. He picked up my case file, read my synopsis, and immediately followed me out the door. He said, "Hey Patch, let's go for a walk". He knew what I had just heard was difficult for me to process. He had also just finished with a disturbing case and needed to get away for a few minutes. When overpowered by a case, we were encouraged to take a break, maybe a short walk. It was expected and never questioned.

We walked down the Marina toward the "pit", past what was left of the Winter Garden, which stood as a glass shell of what it was before the attack. The Winter Garden was the path through which many body bags journeyed, dragged by rescuers and stored in waiting refrigerated trucks for identification. We walked past the mini-mall that was set up in three open sided tents for the rescue personnel to replenish their supplies of clothing, boots, masks, and sundries, all free of charge. We boarded the *Spirit of New York* for a hot lunch. As we joined the other workers, we hardly spoke to each other. We sat with a young Marine and a haggard looking man from the Coast Guard, who kept pushing food around on his plate with his fork. As I ate, I looked out the window of the ship. The view of the river was beautiful with skyscrapers hugging the opposite shore of New Jersey. As long as we didn't look toward the Trade Center, it wasn't too bad. Only the Coast

Guard vessels were on the Hudson with their machine guns guarding the river; normal traffic had not yet returned. The Statue of Liberty stood with her torch held high at the entrance to the Hudson, and when I looked at her I wondered what liberties we were going to lose. What despicable maniacs had imposed this terror on us?

After lunch, we briefly stopped at a flower-laden memorial for the dead rescue workers. The memorial was in an open tent where the photographs of the victims were displayed on ply board. In front of the boards were piles of white lilies, pink baby carnations, and red and yellow roses, cards from all over the country, and teddy bears. The same faces stared out at us that we had seen over and over again, pictures of the courageous dead from the fire and police departments. We stood for a while in silence and respect, and then instead of going down the Marina we went around the buildings behind the shattered Winter Garden. There were no residents in the Red Zone, only military, police, fire, rescue personnel, a few disaster relief workers, and clergy. There was a massive, dirty and tattered American flag still hanging from the front of one of the mammoth-sized damaged structures. The buildings had blown out windows with huge steel pieces of the facades hanging off, as if groping for a hand to pull them back together. To give you an idea of the size, the piece of steel bent over protruding from the side of the building if straightened would be about six stories in height. One of the buildings looked as if a giant can opener had attacked it. The window glass precariously perched and occasionally dropped to the ground endangering everyone working there. In case of death or dismemberment, several workers had drawn their social security numbers on their arms. It was a constant reminder of the danger of the job. Green netting covered some of the buildings to control the continual falling glass. The putrid odor of death swirled through the air, mixing it with the carcinogenic soup that was going to cause health problems for us in the future.

As we walked along a petite female soldier in camouflage fatigues with ash covered combat boots stepped in front of us to prevent us from crossing at the corner. We had to wait. A motorcade was coming down the narrow street squeezing between large parked military trucks. The ash covered trucks appeared to have come out of a desert sandstorm. I leaned against a recently parked vehicle to keep warm, and waited. I thought it was dignitaries visiting the site, but as the small procession started toward us, I knew it wasn't. First there were two police motorcycles, then a silent ambulance known here by the fire department as a "bus" and behind that were two more motorcycles and another ambulance. As they slowly passed us with their red lights flashing and no sirens, an eerie silence shrouded the entire scene; the soldiers and police saluted and stood at attention. Henry was so upset; he saluted with the wrong hand. The older, seasoned police officer standing next to me stepped closer and said, just above a whisper in a thick New York accent, "It's the bodies of twenty-six firemen that were found in a collapsed stairwell this morning." Tears welled up in my eyes, as I forced a sob to stall in my throat. I felt a halo of dignity surrounding the small procession. Two young soldiers standing at attention across the narrow street had tears flowing through the caked ash on their faces. Perhaps, they too had seen too much at the site. The insidious climate of the "pile" created an intense sensitivity to emotional stress. All our nerves were frayed. The disaster, at that instant, moved from a dreamlike surreal state in my mind to reality slapping me right across the face. Henry didn't speak and neither did I. It was a heart wrenching experience, but I knew at least the families of those courageous men would not have to wait and wonder any longer as to the fate of their loved ones. Henry walked about a block ahead of me, as we returned to work. He was crying and trying to get control of his emotions. At that moment we both needed to be alone. I was glad for a little space because I had to clear my head in order to return to work and remain strong in front of my clients. I kept wondering what had led me to this place at this time. I had become a humanitarian worker because our river, the Russian River in Sonoma County, California, had flooded three years previous and I responded to an appeal on the radio asking the public to please call the Red Cross and volunteer in the disaster effort. During that response I not only worked but watched in wonder at how many lives we affected. I decided to continue with the organization and eventually ended up here.

When we returned to the apartment building, our team only did about fifteen cases, and I did none. My job at that point was to bring in clients. I talked to people on the streets and heard stories, each one more tragic than the last. I would tell the clients that we had a person they could speak with who had some good suggestions involving stress and anxiety, but our mental health worker often was busy, and when someone started to talk to me, they couldn't seem to stop. In a strange way they would attach themselves to me, or another worker, and refuse to speak to anyone else. So we listened and their words coated our souls with a tremendous sadness.

I spoke to a tall dark-haired woman with her child in a stroller, who showed photos her husband had taken as the cataclysmic event took place. They were incredible, showing the buildings collapsing as debris, ash, and cement spewed from a tsunami type cloud that erupted from the impact of the jets. She told me she and her husband had excellent jobs, had been evacuated from their $4,000 a month apartment in Battery Park, and were afraid to go back. They were temporarily living in a hotel and rapidly going through their savings, and had maxed out their credit cards. She would have to continue paying her lease despite the fact that the family could no longer live in the unit. She was entitled to a family grant and a disbursing order for food because there was no electricity in her apartment, and all of their food had spoiled. We also were able to pay her rent and maintenance fees. She seemed to be a proud person and had never in her lifetime been in a position that forced her to ask for assistance. I explained it was a gift from the American people and that made it easier for her. I brought her into the building and introduced her to one of our caseworkers. While the family service worker was writing up her case, I sat with her little four-year-old girl. She was a stunning child with a precocious personality. Her shinny black hair was tied back with a blue satin ribbon that matched her eyes. She had several freckles rolling over her tiny nose and a dark beauty mark kissed her rosy cheek. We colored, and she warmed right up to me. When the young mother finished, she came over and told me that the child was standing at their apartment window that looked out on the World Trade Center when the jets veered into the buildings.

The child began to vomit and, since the incident, anytime there was an unusually loud noise she would vomit.

Right after the attack the mother left immediately to retrieve her other child, who was close by in a daycare/preschool. She grabbed her little girl, her purse, and stuffed their yowling Siamese cat into a carrier, and left for the school. In the meantime, the police had evacuated the daycare children, putting them on a boat and shipping them to New Jersey. The woman told me of the terror of not knowing where her family was located, and her struggle to find them in all the chaos around her.

When the woman left with her daughter, I decided to stay inside long enough to get warm. As I settled down at my table to do some casework, a lovely Asian woman with her son in tow came in seeking our help. The toddler was very nervous, jumping at ever noise, and hiding behind his mother's leg. The mother wasn't home when the incident occurred, and a good thing it was too because the shock blew out her windows and the apartment was a foot deep in debris, glass, asbestos, cement, and body parts. The incident had ravished her home. Her older son was in the school nearby. The school evacuated the children to the edge of the Hudson River on the other side of the playground. With tears streaming down her face, the mother revealed to me that the children all stood there, and witnessed the people throwing themselves out of the windows of the Trade Center building. "You must understand that my boy is a sensitive child. He can't sleep and wets his bed every night. What am I to do?" She was grateful that we had a mental health worker she could speak with. How would the children ever recover, or would they? I had no answers because I didn't understand myself why all of this happened to all of these innocent people.

2 October 2001 - Tuesday
Manhattan, New York

I got up early and tried to read, but couldn't focus on anything, but my job. As soon as I got to the Chapter in Brooklyn, I went downstairs to the cafeteria, and ate some cereal, and then off to the staff meeting after which our team gathered in the park outside for a brief meeting where we discussed our strategy for the day in an attempt to go into the Red Zone with some sense of organization and a plan. Usually with all the chaos things changed almost instantly. I think we were all groping for normalcy. We left headquarters to our destination, the Red Zone. The weather had taken a pleasant change and the winds died down, thank God. We arrived at our makeshift office where I began to prepare for the arrival of our clients. I was stacking small boxes of supplies, extracting what pamphlets I thought we might need for the day, when I looked out at the river. I saw to my surprise the white hospital ship *U.S.S Comfort*, which was pulling out of the harbor. Fireboats sent up great sprays of water bidding her farewell, and thanking her for her presence in the wake of the terrorist attack. She was the only ship on the river, which magnified her beauty. It was a splendid sight, a ship well named bringing comfort to our wounded nation. It had come to assist the injured, but the vast majority of the people were dead or missing. The sunshine created the illusion of rainbows in the spray, the ancient symbol of God's mercy, something we all clung to on a daily basis both in the Yellow and Red Zones.

After the ship passed out of view I left the lobby to look for clients on the streets, but I couldn't find any. Men on hoists were washing the buildings, and were as high as thirty stories. It made me uneasy because they were washing all sorts of dust and dirt down on me. Maybe that was why most people were not on the streets. I talked to the police, the Marines, and then to a group of men that worked in the apartment building across the street, who was sitting outside smoking. One younger man told me his father was a supervisor for an investment firm on the 55th floor of Tower Two. After the plane hit, his father telephoned the family on his cell phone telling them he was all right, but that there had been an announcement for people to stay in their offices. He obeyed. It was a fatal error that cost him his life, and left a wife without a husband and two teenagers without their beloved father.

I went back and asked my more experienced coworker, Jack, about the family, and he told me to have the man come over to speak with him. I went back across the street and relayed Jack's request. The young man told me he would be over in about an hour, but he didn't show up. So, I took the nurse and went to see him again. He finally came to the lobby. He was Hispanic, about eighteen-years-old, and now the head of the family. He was a tall, thin, and handsome man, visibly shaken and nervous addressing me in a wobbly, muted voice.

I have always worked on teams, but this time teamwork was so evident, and it was a wonderful feeling. Our mental health worker spoke to the young man. Then Jack, the worker from a respite center, and a new member of our team sat and talked to him. We pulled out the stops for the widows and orphans of the Trade Center. We did all the work on one sheet of paper. There was no paperwork available for what we were doing. None of this had ever happened before. We paid three months rent, funeral expenses, bills, car payments, insurance, just about everything including three months of food and utilities. [The financial assistance increased considerably as time went on.] The young man's family had a great need, so I told him to bring his mother to our location the next day.

I went deeper into the Red Zone that afternoon to assist an outreach team at South End. They needed another Family Service caseworker because they were shorthanded. The building was one more wounded giant skyscraper. An attractive landscaped area between the buildings gave it a park like appearance, but after the incident it was filthy and covered with layers of dust and small unidentifiable debris. The destructive force had blown out windows and destroyed apartments. The lobby we were to work in was intact, no blown-out windows. Some of the tenants were returning briefly during the day attempting to salvage their belongings. A thick layer of ash coated everything, giving the entire lobby a dirty gray appearance. It hadn't been cleaned and we were breathing the dust, and God knows what else. My lungs hurt and I felt like I had pneumonia. My eyes watered and my nose ran. I tried to wear a mask when I was outside, but when I interviewed clients it inhibited my communication skills. We were still stuck with the thin white paper masks, which were totally useless.

There were only nine caseworkers at the site with two supervisors, four nurses, and two mental health professionals. I thanked God that I was a Disaster Action Team leader at home because the experience proved invaluable. I was skilled at dealing with near-hysterical clients. I was used to working under adverse conditions, but the location of the apartment building was the worst environment I had ever worked in.

While I was working, Paula, my Disaster Director from home, called and when I answered she wasn't there. I was my new cell phone's worst enemy, often pushing the incorrect button. I was fortunate having come from a Chapter that showed the utmost concern about my well-being.

I stuffed my cell phone in my vest pocket and went to work in our makeshift office of unsteady card tables and whatever chairs we could scrounge. We put a variety of teddy bears all along the windows to give to the clients. The bears brought comfort to the children, as well as the adults. If I interviewed a woman who was particularly upset and gave her a bear, she would clutch it as if it were an all important child, often rocking back and forth as she told her story.

The noise level was intense, conversations echoing off the tall ceilings of the lobby, and the roar and clatter of trucks rolling by, helicopters coming and going, and heavy equipment that felt like small earthquakes; the noise was a constant. The work went on twenty-four hours a day, and the military presence was intense, along with the usual array of police and fire personnel. We were there as support for them, as well as the people who lived and worked in the area, and they treated us well.

A couple of male detectives dressed in civilian clothing from NYPD came in and talked to me. They just wanted to take a break and were curious why anyone would come all the way from California to help the people in New York City. I explained that we worked all over the United States and that the assault on the buildings was a direct hit on all of us. They told us about the negative affect the attacks had on their children. So, we gave them teddy bears to take home and brochures on what to say to their kids regarding the disaster. They stayed for about an hour watching our operation. One of the detectives was a large man of medium build and at least 6' 3". He was a sight standing there clutching a teddy bear, a gentle giant. The other detective also a large man, but heavy-set reached over and gave me a hug and thanked me for the work I was doing. I felt buried in his arms. At that they left, and told us all to be careful and be safe.

The building we were in was opposite of the Trade Center, and after work we exited the Red Zone from a different position than our last location. It was a long walk out to the checkpoint gate, where men were hosing the pollutants off all the vehicles exiting the Red Zone. They were in white and blue suits that covered their entire bodies, giving them the appearance of astronauts. I wondered what I carried out of the Red Zone because my clothing was contaminated, and at night when I washed out my under garments they left black water in the sink.

Some Marines drove by in a vehicle that had a flat open back. I hitched a ride; they stopped their motorized Land Rover, and generously gave all six of us transport to the checkpoint and waiting security. I had tired feet and welcomed the ride. It had been a long and arduous day for all of us.

3 October 2001 – Wednesday
Manhattan, New York

After a restless night, I got up at 4:30 a.m. and went to the corner grocery to buy a banana for a quick snack. The bus was late, so a van came to pick us up. It only took our small outreach team because we didn't work in Brooklyn, and only needed to go there to pick up our disbursing orders and attend a brief meeting. We had to return to Manhattan on the subway to reach the Red Zone before eight o'clock. If we had waited with the other workers, we would have been late.

The driver was a short, rotund Puerto Rican man, who was wedged between the seat and the steering wheel of a small black van. He had ink black curly hair, a matching moustache, and smelled of expensive shaving lotion and cigars. He kept clearing his throat as he pointed out the sights filling us in on local history. I think he wanted to create a more relaxed atmosphere as we drove past multitudes of heavily armed police and military personnel. The authorities had blocked off many streets and were stopping vehicles to check identifications before allowing people to continue. It was uncomfortable to have the feeling of no freedom, and the large police presence on every street. The soldiers stopped our unmarked vehicle, and our driver took my identification card to get us through. The soldier checked it, and looked into the van, at which he saluted us and told us to be safe. So many thoughts were running through my head. I knew we were walking through the making of history and I also knew we were not safe and perhaps never would be again.

We got to the Chapter late and I didn't have time to eat breakfast, as I ran off to a staff meeting. After the meeting, the outreach teams gathered in the park for another briefing. I asked the supervisor if I could work with his group because I needed to follow the case through about the widow that was due in today. He agreed. That put me a couple of blocks farther from the smoke and into a cleaner building for the day, plus I really wanted to see the case through. There was a great deal to learn. I was so impressed with the teamwork involved around the case. I told the supervisor I was flexible and would go to any location after we processed the widow. That wasn't a problem.

She didn't show up and after a couple of hours, we started making phone calls. We discovered that she couldn't enter the Red Zone because she didn't have the identification necessary to get her by the soldiers. She didn't live or work in the Red Zone. Her son worked there, but that didn't get her in, so we went out to escort her. She met us at the barricades, and we explained to the military personnel who we were and what we were doing. They then let the widow pass. The situation increased the poor woman's stress if that was possible.

She was a bleached blonde Hispanic, well-dressed in a rose colored pant suit with gold jewelry on her ears, arms, and neck. Her chubby fourteen-year-old daughter, a woman child, who was wearing a tight low cut green sweater with short sleeves exposing tattoos on her breast, and DKNY black jeans, came to support her mother. Her lips darkly outlined in ruby pencil, raven black hair, creamy olive skin, and intense brown eyes welled up with tears that slowly escaped to cascade down her round cheeks.

I expressed my condolences for their loss. Jack was closing up with another client, so I spent some time with the family. I took them to a quiet dimly lit corner with a couch, two overstuffed chairs, and a small table. I gave the woman and her teenage daughter teddy bears, and just sat and listened to their account of the attack, and how it had torn her family apart. The widow was trying to be strong, as she told me the story of her best friend's husband who worked on the 66th floor of one of the Towers. As he was making his escape, a fireball that burned sixty-percent of his body hit him. In spite of that, he had somehow gotten out of the building. His wife began a gallant hunt to find her spouse by putting up fliers, searching respite centers and hospitals to no avail. She knew he was alive and her persistent hunt led her to him. He was among the unidentified, burned beyond recognition, except for a small birthmark on his ankle that was intact. She knew she had found her husband. So being inspired by her friend, my client knew she would find her husband too.

The widow sat there clutching a death certificate, nervously running her fingers over the edges, as if trying to make the word homicide disappear. He was not going to be found anywhere, except under mountainous piles of debris. Her husband had been taken from her, and the daughter, who was the sister to the young man I met on the street.

The formalities were simple, all done on one sheet of paper called the Family Emergency Grant. The woman took out several envelopes from her large leather purse and spread them out on the table like a little child's favorite collection of small toys. The conversation with the family was difficult. The family's dilemma filled me with sorrow and compassion for their circumstances. We talked about death and reality, while she sat there in a state of denial, making every attempt to stay composed and in control. We paid everything in three-month increments. We gave her monies for expenses such as gas, water, garbage, and food. We took care of her credit cards, rent, payments, and any other bills she had buried in her big envelopes. The most difficult for me was when we allocated $8,000 for funeral expenses. We discussed with her that if the body wasn't recovered there would still be a memorial, and it would be expensive. We had to talk about details, which was painful for all of us. She didn't shed a tear, but the pain was imprinted on deep creases running along her face. I just held her hand and let her talk, while I mostly listened, and her daughter whose face was red and swollen from crying, gently rubbed her mother's back. It was a tough job to talk to a woman whose husband had disappeared under tons and tons of concrete. She showed me his photograph, which made it all the more real. He was a forty-nine-year old businessman with dark bushy black hair, an olive complexion, and a small black moustache. He had a smile on his face and his eyes sparkled with fun. The son had told us before that his father had phoned from the office during the attack. She told us too that her husband had telephoned her when the first plane hit reassuring her that everything was going to be fine. We spent two difficult hours with the mother and daughter, and I found it hard to remain strong in front of them, but I did. I was so tired and drained when we were done that there was nothing left of me, but I knew we had given them valuable assistance and hopefully relieved at least some of their stress.

After the family left, Jack and I went to the *Spirit of New York,* and we knew that it being an off hour, the ship wouldn't be crowded. It was late afternoon as we walked along the river promenade and past the Winter Garden to clear our minds. We boarded the ship and went to the dining area. We hardly spoke to each other as we ate. After lunch, we decided to go to the top deck. The smoke was so thick that it covered the city, but in both the Yellow and Red Zones it was like a blanket covering my lungs. It hurt my eyes and throat. I was beginning to find it difficult to inhale. We met a tall, dark-haired, middle-aged Catholic priest with a gas mask tied to his belt. We chatted, but not about what we were all going through. We talked for fifteen minutes about our homes, and families, and his parish. It was a nice break, but we all knew we had to return to our jobs, so we said goodbye and the priest told us to be safe as he headed back toward the "pile".

When we returned, I was saddened to learn that two of our mental health team members were leaving the Red Zone. The stress was more than they could handle. I was surprised because I saw no sign of it. The two of them went to work at headquarters in Brooklyn. The Red Zone was extremely emotional and difficult work requiring nerves of steel, and it wasn't suited to everyone; actually it wasn't suited to anyone.

That afternoon we began short two workers, but it wasn't too busy, so we managed. A tall, thin woman with beautiful shoulder length golden-brown hair that fell over a pink cashmere jacket came in to see us. She was distraught and appeared to still be in shock. I started working with her and realized I needed assistance, but there were only three of us in the spacious lobby and no mental health worker. I asked Joe, a caseworker, where Michael was. He was our only remaining mental health individual on our team and he wasn't on the premises. Joe said, "You handle it", so I did. We talked for a long time, and as she began to trust me she related her story. It seemed to me that I mostly listened and gave her one-hundred percent of my attention.

In the near vicinity of the Trade Center were two schools, a grammar school and Stuyvesant High School on Chambers Street. The woman was volunteering in a classroom at the grammar school as a parent-aid when the first plane hit. Her small group of disabled students, who were all young, began to cry when they realized what had happened. She related that she could hear the high school students screaming. The second plane hit, and she knew they were in serious trouble, but wasn't sure what action to take. Daylight became darkness when the buildings collapsed and terror gripped their hearts. There was dust everywhere, flying concrete, paper, and glass. The woman gathered her flock, hoping to get them out of the building and to safety. She never mentioned where the teacher had gone, and I didn't ask her because I didn't want to interrupt her story. She could hardly see as her world filled with dust and ash. She was terrified, but she managed to herd the young children to the nearby edge of the Hudson River picking them up as she went dragging, prodding, and pulling them along with her. When she got the hysterical children to the riverside, she kept herding them trying to keep them all together. The authorities evacuated the children and her by boat to New Jersey.

The woman's blue eyes filled with tears as she continued to speak. They slid down her ashen cheeks. She wiped them away in one sweep of her hand. That the children had to endure such an ordeal left her full of guilt because she was powerless to have made it easier for them. I told her she was a heroine, and that I would be proud to have a friend like her. The courage the woman displayed completely amazed me. She, like many other people on that day, risked her own life to save others, but she was among the lucky because she survived. I opened a case giving her all that I could, and suggested she speak with our mental health professional. I never referred to them as mental health, but I usually told the clients that we had workers who had good advice on stress and how to move forward from disaster, and would they like to speak with them. I told her our mental health worker would be back shortly. She refused to speak to the worker and stayed for about forty-five minutes talking to me. When she got up to leave, I gave her a big hug and wished her luck in the future. I also gave her a bear and she left thanking me. I admired her courage so much and wondered if I could be that brave, if the occasion were to arise. The responsibility of not being able to get my client to mental health weighed heavily on me. I didn't have the training our pros had, and all I could offer the woman was compassion, love and the ability to sincerely listen to her story. I worried about that when the occasion occurred, when the clients refused to leave me.

My last client of the day was a young Hungarian man with dirty blond hair and green eyes. He had come to the building to try to clean his apartment, but was sure it wasn't safe and he said he knew the air was dangerous. The management had cleaned the apartment, but he was convinced it was a bad environment for his newborn baby. I gave him groceries, and a Family Assistance Grant, but it didn't end there. He told me that on September 11, he and his wife and young son had taken a morning stroll near the Trade Center. The weather was beautiful and they were enjoying their daily exercise. His wife was due and waiting for their unborn child to arrive. They were new in America and looking forward to a full and happy future. That sunny morning they witnessed the first plane hit the tower and thought it was a terrible accident, until the second hit, and then they knew it was no accident. He had taken his video camera to record his young son and wife on their morning outing. His camera quickly turned to the Towers. The incident fascinated them, until the towers collapsed, at which time they picked up their child and ran for their lives not being able to see through the tsunami of dust and debris, as the world turned dark and life, as they knew it disappeared. He begged me for information to help his traumatized wife and son. He didn't know what to do, so I sent him to talk to Michael who had returned to the lobby along with giving him our literature on how to understand trauma in young children after a disaster, and all sorts of references where he could get more assistance for his wife.

We left the building at 7:30 p.m. and walked to the outer edge of the Red Zone. There were still nothing but emergency vehicles in the area, and the air quality hadn't improved, at least in my opinion. There was so much smoke, and dust, and the smell clung to my clothes and stayed in my memory after I left the site. My eyes were red and bloodshot, but I blamed that on the constant cold wind hitting me in the face. There was such a drastic temperature difference when we entered the subway from the street above. It was stifling to the point of being uncomfortable.

We made good time getting to Brooklyn. When I finished checking in my disbursing orders, I took the Chapter bus back to Manhattan to the hotel. There was a message on my telephone. A woman from my Chapter who was in New York invited me to the opening night at Carnegie Hall, which was across the street from our Park Central hotel, but I didn't have the clothing for opening night anywhere. My clothes were appropriate for maybe a boxing match. In addition, I was extremely tired and knew I would fall asleep half way through the concert. New York was a hospitable city and they were issuing tickets to the "heroes" for all of the shows, musicals, and plays for a mere $25. Most of the people went out at night, but I couldn't. Besides suffering physical and emotional exhaustion, I was trying to process the tragedy that I had become a part of, definitely not leaving me in a party mood.

I felt that on this particular assignment, I had to eat right, and if possible get to bed before eleven. Even at that I wasn't getting eight hours sleep. Our bus didn't get back to the hotel till 9:30 p.m. sometimes even later. The job was demanding on my mind and I didn't think I could serve my clients at the level they deserved, if I was too tired. I had no idea how tired I really was. They needed intense attention, and I needed to do the best I could to be totally present to them, to be compassionate and understanding, but somewhere in all this I forgot to be compassionate to myself.

4 October 2001 – Thursday
Manhattan, New York

What a way to start a day! I was not sleeping well at night because I was having nightmares. I woke up around 3:00 a.m. and couldn't go back to sleep, so I just stayed in bed and tried to rest. At 4:30 a.m. I decided to go to the deli down the block to buy a banana, so I could get change to put on the pillow for the hotel maid, who made up my room daily. The man in the deli said in broken English, "Sixty cents for the banana." I said, "How come! Yesterday they were forty cents." He said, "You bought a bigger banana." It was the same grocer who wanted fifty-seven cents for the thirty-four cent stamps. Needless to say, I didn't buy the banana, and made the decision to change my morning routine. Who could handle such a dialogue at that hour of the day?

I took off to work on the subway, so I could get the route down. I didn't want to try to get from Brooklyn to the hotel on the day I was going to leave for home, and get lost. I was on edge when I rode the Metro. I was convinced that if there were another terrorist attack it would be in the subway. There were thousands of people down there. There were miles of tunnels and the exits were narrow stairs, or single person escalators. If people panicked, they would never get out. If you got stuck in a tunnel or on a train, you would be completely out of luck. Besides worrying about that, every day on the news and in the neighborhood, we heard of a new anthrax case and the possibility of plague, small pox and chemical gasses. Despite all of that thinking, I had an uneventful ride to Brooklyn.

When I got to the headquarters, I went downstairs to eat some breakfast. The Mass Care staff had moved a television into the cafeteria, so everyone could see the latest news, and the updates on what action the politicians were planning. I went to Records and Reports and got my disbursing orders for the day, and then headed to the daily staff meeting. After we met in the park as usual, our team was off to the subway station.

As we approached the Red Zone, I began to process the thoughts of how horrible it was that I was growing accustomed to the military presence, checkpoints, and fear on an everyday basis. When we exited the subway, the smoke was incredibly offensive, and most of our team was wearing the paper thin white masks. I passed a young woman on the street who was coughing uncontrollably. I was wearing a mask and she came up to me and asked me if she could have it. I usually kept extras in my carry on bag, but I had given so many away that I didn't have a spare, but offered her mine. She was so desperate that she took the dirty mask off my face, a face she didn't even know. As she slipped it over her blonde hair down onto her face, she thanked me profusely. She appeared to be asthmatic, and I was afraid she was going to keel over right in front of me. I touched her shoulder and said, "Things will get better. Hang in there." She smiled, turned and walked up the street with what sounded like a deadly cough. Before I came to New York City I would have shied away from anyone coughing like that but it was now a common sound in any crowd.

We arrived at the dirty and cold lobby wondering what the day was going to bring us. The building manager said he wanted to get back to normal and that our presence reminded people of the disaster – not that they couldn't look out their windows and see it every moment. He wanted us to find another location.

I heard the same sad stories as people came in and sat down at our tables, often crying or just numb and still in shock. The rescue personnel pulled out more bodies today and the smell was dreadful. I talked to everyone who entered the building and informed them as to why we were there, and so many people applied for assistance. We notified them we were going to move from the building, but that we would still be available to them at a different location. On every job I had been on, Red Cross never just pulled out without notifying the people at least 24-hours beforehand. I was hoping that our new location would possibly be cleaner, but then we were still in the Red Zone and clean wasn't possible.

After a twelve hour workday, we left and returned to headquarters. First, I turned in my paperwork and prepared to leave for the evening, when a staff member gave me a new Red Cross sweatshirt, for which I was grateful because the weather was getting colder and all I had was my Red Cross jacket. My new coat proved too bulky to wear under my uniform apron. I wasn't going to take the Red Cross bus back to the hotel, but was determined to find my way alone on the subway. I was wearing my Red Cross jacket with the new sweatshirt underneath and felt so much warmer. As I was getting off the crowded train at 59th Street, a man leaned over and grabbed my hand and pressed something into it. Strangely enough he didn't scare me. His touch was gentle, but firm, and his eyes so sad. I exited the train and looked down into my palm to find a small package with a tiny American flag pin. He reaffirmed my presence in Manhattan and at Ground Zero. I knew I belonged there doing the work I was doing.

5 October 2001 – Friday
Ground Zero, New York

The usual routine in the morning, I caught the 5:30 a.m. bus to the Chapter, had breakfast, and went to the staff meeting. I specifically asked at the meeting if they had any reports on the air quality in the Red Zone. They said not to worry about it, and that it was just dirty and wouldn't have any long term affects on us. The air quality reports were inconsistent, and I was becoming concerned because my lungs hurt, and I had developed a nasty cough. I didn't feel ill, but I just couldn't get rid of the persistent cough.

When we arrived at work, Henry, our supervisor, told us we would be finishing up at our present location because the apartment manager wanted us to leave, which we all knew. They had been very courteous to us, but we needed to find a new location. Henry and I walked across the wide street littered with hoses and military equipment to another apartment building. The thoroughly cleaned lobby was pleasant with big plants, and a glistening pink marble front desk, behind which stood an immaculately groomed doorman and clerk. It was hard to believe this place was in the Red Zone. It had sustained no visible damage. Henry went to the manager's office to request permission to set up in the building. I stayed in the lobby and talked to a heavy-set elderly Italian woman. She had short white hair and glasses with thick lenses that perched on the bridge of her large nose and was linked to clothing under her coat by a shining silver chain. She was sitting on a beige French provincial style couch looking quite comfortable. Her walker was propped up against a nearby chair. Placed on an inlayed rosewood coffee table was a lovely silver plated tea set from which the woman offered me refreshments. She was delighted to have someone to tell her story to. Everyone had a story and everyone wanted to tell it. I came to believe that it was part of the healing process they were all going through. She told me the day of the incident was so traumatic for her. She was terrified that she would die, so she left the building trying to get to the waterfront which was just up the street and down a set of stairs. The older woman twisted her pearls and wiped the palms of her hands up and down the front of her cashmere coat as she continued speaking. She had left her walker and run out of sheer terror. Since then she had to increase her pain medications, and was almost unable to walk. She had done considerable damage to her pain-wracked body, but she was alive and had no intentions of moving out of her apartment. She was pleased that there was a Red Cross presence in the neighborhood, although she stated that she didn't need our assistance. It made her feel like everything was going to be all right. We chatted until Henry was ready to leave, at which I said goodbye and wished her good luck. She replied, "Be safe and be careful, my dear." I was beginning to think that was a neighborhood mantra and that it would soon be appearing on tee-shirts. The manager refused Henry's request, but was extremely polite in thanking us for being available to the people.

We returned and I processed three clients before lunchtime, and then Henry and I walked to the *Spirit of New York.* It was the last day that the ship would be available to the rescue personnel for meals. The new respite facilities for us were at the Marriott Financial Center. I knew the next day I would be working at a new location somewhere else in the Red Zone, and probably wouldn't have been able to get to the ship anyway.

After lunch, I had a client that told me they had found her brother or at least part of him and had done DNA testing to confirm the fact that it was he. He worked high up in the Trade Center and never got out. It was interesting and tragic to observe that some cultures put an enormous importance on recovering a body to bury. The cases went on with the same disastrous affects on every family involved.

In the late afternoon, my supervisor told two of us to take an extra large cardboard box of teddy bears farther into the Red Zone to a makeshift service center near Battery Park. I was glad to go for a walk and not have to deal with clients for a while. Ruth and I struggled down the block in the wind juggling our large box, when we saw two motorcycles and a police car go by with their lights on, driving slowly and removing more body parts from the scene. It just went on and on. There was no place I could turn without tragedy, sorrow, and pain. Our box was big and awkward, so we stopped to rest for a few minutes, and spoke to a Salvation Army crew, who had set up a tent along our route. They had sundries, candy, Christian literature, and water for anyone who needed it. They were a great group of people, very kind and dedicated. Our box was broken and they helped us tape it. A small bear fell out onto the street, and I picked him up and put him into my work vest pocket with just his little brown face hanging out. He never left that pocket the entire time I worked at Ground Zero. Even the most upset clients would see him and smile. After enjoying a bottle of water, we went on with our repaired box. The police smiled as we passed and greeted us warmly. After we delivered the bears, we returned to our workplace and more waiting clients. The Red Zone was a larger area than people realized (280 acres) and the full size couldn't be seen on television, but we definitely got our exercise going from one place to another. It was a long day and I was tired, and my lungs hurt.

After we returned to Brooklyn, I took the train home alone and didn't get lost. One of my coworkers said when you started calling the hotel home it was time to leave. The subway train was crowded with people pressed against one another making it difficult to see the stops. I finally arrived at Lincoln Circle, where I surfaced and walked a few blocks to Park Central. The streets were well planned and easy to follow, but so crowded that it looked like everyone was Christmas shopping. Of course, they weren't; it was just the regular crowded streets of midtown Manhattan.

When I returned to the hotel, I telephoned my husband. It was 9:00 p.m. New York time, making it rather early in California. I was lucky he was still in the office. He was glad to hear from me and it was good to hear a voice from home. We talked briefly, and then I took a hot shower and went right to bed. I took a sleeping pill, hoping to derail the nightmares and get an uninterrupted night's sleep. I was too tired to eat.

6 October 2001 – Saturday
Ground Zero, New York

It was pouring rain with howling winds whipping around the skyscrapers. The rain came down on a slant driving us into the damaged buildings. I worked with a group of ten at a place that was even deeper into the recover operation area. The weather matched the gloomy mood of the people involved in the mess. Despite my taking a sleeping pill last night, I had nightmares about planes crashing into my home in California. I was sure it was because I heard the story over and over again about the planes hitting the Trade Center. Every TV played the scene non-stop day after day. I was visually overwhelmed.

I figured we would be busy, but wasn't sure how the New Yorkers would react to the rain and the cold, which didn't seem to bother them in the least. The culture was very different than at home. I liked the people and found them to be tough, resilient, and friendly toward me. After the meeting in Brooklyn we took off for the Zone.

We worked in another apartment lobby that had big windows on each side that went from the floor to the ceiling about thirty feet up. One side was a view of beautiful birch trees, the other a park like walkway that wound around the building, which stood tight next to the other buildings like soldiers in an army. They stood tall near to the rubble of the World Trade Center, as if in respect for their fallen comrades. They stunk like soldiers in battle too long, but the wind blew hard, and for short periods pushed the smell away.

There was a constant stream of clients with similar stories – all tragic, some worse than others. But, upstairs in her apartment was a young woman from Haiti with a three-year-old child. Her husband had gone to his office early on September 11th to catch up on some work. There was no recovery of the body. The authorities gave the widow a death certificate. Henry was waiting for Michael to bring the woman to the lobby, so we could assist her with her finances. He knew it would be some time before she would come down, so he suggested John and I walk to the Marriott to eat lunch. The hotel was located in the Red Zone and was the new feeding location with hot meals, snacks, places to rest.

When we approached the hotel it was from an angle I hadn't seen, and there was a large remaining piece of the Tower about ten stories in height sticking up through the muck, window frames looked like burned mouths gaping at the tragedy. Someone had tied an American flag on a nearby badly damaged building, and the wind had torn it giving it the appearance of a bullet riddled, filthy battle flag. All sizes of American flags were scattered around Ground Zero many hung from buildings. We Americans marked our territory screaming out in protest for the assault on our homeland. The mountain of debris was still smoking and the fire was still burning. The nearby buildings were damaged ghosts with windows out and cement dust, fiberglass, plastics, and asbestos still blowing throughout the structures. The remains before me were a skeletal glimpse into hell. Death, destruction, and sadness wrapped their arms around us smothering us with every breath. Large trucks had massive tan fire hoses lying all over the street, creating a network of obstacles to walk over and around to get into the Marriott. We entered the respite by the side door having to pass through a wash rack where we hosed off our shoes, and scrubbed our hands at a long line of about nine sinks that were attached to the façade of the building. The hotel had plastic covering on all the rugs, but the floors were covered with dirt and smelled like everywhere in the Zone. The pulverized dirt in the Zone crept into everything; not even the plastic kept it out. Two Mass Care Red Cross workers greeted us. They checked us in, asked us to sign a sheet of paper that stated who we were, and the time of our arrival. After we checked in, we went up what once was a beautiful, wide staircase, now covered with dirt and plastic to a hall lined with serving tables full of hot roast beef, roasted potatoes, fresh steamed green beans, rice, and fried chicken, snacks, and milk, juices, and cokes. The Red Cross was serving the food and the skyscraper had become a respite center. [The Marriott was later torn down because it was not structurally sound. We weren't safe anywhere.]

We went into the dimly-lit dining room, which was also dirty, but there were clean linens on the tables with cards from school children from every imaginable location in the country. I ate with John and a couple of firemen at a big round table that could have seated at least twelve people easily. At the next table sat huge, muscular men in recovery gear. They wore enormous hooks attached to body harnesses and bandanas wrapped around their heads. They were members of a police department rescue squad. There was little conversation and everyone looked extremely tired, many with that frozen stare I had become so familiar with. John was a small, older man and looked stunted next to the other men in the room.

There were two firemen eating at the other adjacent table, or I should say talking over two dishes of food. One of the men was crying. I moved to their table and asked if I could get them some help and he blurted out a story I would have rather not heard. Apparently, this morning they had found two adult hands clutching the remains of a baby. I had heard nothing about children killed in the Zone. He was devastated, having young kids of his own. He said what was going to happen: everyone was dead, everyone. He was beyond exhaustion and at this point only recovering the most grizzly of finds. No matter how tired, they weren't going to leave one "brother" or civilian unaccounted for, so they continued their work. I began to feel that every story was accumulating in my brain, eating me alive. My lack of safety ran through my mind continually. I was thinking as I looked at all the rescue and relief personnel present realizing they couldn't protect us. No one could anymore. We were vulnerable and tired and trying our best to deal with what the terrorist left behind.

I rejoined John as he was finishing his lunch. We were both anxious to leave, concerned about the Haitian woman and knew we needed to be there when she came down. As we left the hotel and began our walk back I turned and looked once more at the skeletal remains of one of the Towers and my mind snapped a picture that permanently took its place in my psyche, a place of intense pain. When we returned the woman had not come down yet.

The afternoon was chaotic as people streamed in for assistance. A middle-aged couple from Sweden sat before me, and I handled their case. They were both journalists and came to New York to write for a Swedish newspaper. They worked in their apartment that looked out onto the World Trade Center, and were home at the time of the incident. There seven-year-old son saw everything, including the people jumping out of the buildings. The child had asthma, and the incident had caused it to escalate to a point that he was always having difficulty breathing. I wasn't sure if it was from trauma, or the rotten air we were all exposed to on a daily basis. The family had lost everything and requested our assistance. They had their windows open during the attack and dust and debris covered the entire contents of their apartment. They were the saddest people because it was an absolute that they didn't know what to do, and at that point didn't seem capable of making any decisions about their future. All they could tell me over and over again was how great life had been for them in America, and now their dreams were shattered. The attack had traumatized the family. The woman was in total shock, the husband was petrified with fear, and the child was paying for what he saw or breathed in short gasping wheezes. I gave them what assistance I could and Michael talked with them for quite a while. The man came back and gave me a hug before they left and asked me to pray for them.

I worked with another two clients, and then decided to take a short break. As I left the makeshift office I noticed seven gray squirrels running, chasing each other in circular panic. They squealed and ran frightened looking for food, but there was nothing but ash and contaminated dirt. I couldn't understand where they came from. I asked a police officer who was passing by and he told me they were fed by the people who lived in the area. They had nothing to live on except the pieces of bread the people fed them daily. In normal times nannies would walk their charges or push baby buggies and stop to feed the squirrels. It was a daily ritual. The little animals were domesticated. Older tenants of the area would sit on the benches and feed them, just having the pleasure of watching them beg. Now hungry lost cats stalked them. I looked on them with pity thinking they would surely die. There was nothing in or around Ground Zero that wasn't suffering. It made me angry and sad.

I had to wear a mask and battle freezing cold wind to cross the park like courtyard, and enter a badly damaged unoccupied building where the only available bathroom was located. By the time I reached it, my mask was filled with cement dust. Between the buildings the wind was so strong that it nearly blew me over, and I had to walk on a slant just to stay upright. I went down three dozen sets of concrete stairs supported by cracked walls to finally reach the ladies' room. Lights weren't on in the main building but the staircase was dimly lit. In the bathroom stalls one toilet was in pieces and covered with a blue tarp. The other was filthy and covered with some kind of green slime and dust. Both stall doors looked like someone kicked them in and were just hanging to the side. There was a green mold on the walls that created a smell making it difficult to breathe. I felt as if my body was being compressed, crushed when I would inhale. It was a creepy building because it was deserted, and I felt isolated and unsafe going there alone. I tried not to go there, unless it was absolutely necessary.

As I was walking back to the lobby of the apartment building I spotted in the bushes what I thought was a dead kitten. I leaned over to investigate and discovered a decomposing hand of a human being. There was a gold wedding band on the ring finger, a finger partially missing. My heart sank and I felt ice cold all over. I passed the apartment lobby door and went directly out onto the street and told a man in army fatigues that was standing guard over something in front of a cyclone fence. He summoned some workers who responded with a white bucket removing the body part. I knew the buildings were also full of body parts that just hadn't been found yet. That was hard for me and I kept it to myself.

When I returned from the bathroom, I was to spend the next hour briefing our Americorps volunteers, training them on how to correctly do the paperwork. I always enjoyed associating with them because they worked hard and had wonderful attitudes. They were always willing to learn. After I finished with my last Americorps girl, I went to assist a client. My mind couldn't clear the picture of the hand, but I forced myself to put it aside so I could work.

The client was a small, arrogant man with a big, mean attitude. The receptionist sent the middle-aged man, and his shy, silent partner to my table. They were my last clients of the day, and had been to Red Cross before. I had to call headquarters to find out what we had already given them. They wanted seven days added to their hotel, and normally that would have been okay, but all the crabby man did was gripe and demand. I called the hotel and they told me they were staying in a room for $200 per night, so I requested a rate, and negotiated with the clerk getting the price down to $175. Then I found out the hotel had similar rooms for $85 a night, and told the client we would prefer he downscale because we had to be good stewards of the monies we were handling. The man screamed and called me names, threatened me to a point that I called Henry over to be of assistance. We agreed to pay $85 per day partial, and they could stay in their room, if they were willing to make up the difference. He was the most horrible man, but I was very nice to him and very patient. After several telephone calls, the supervisor came back to my table and approved not just seven days, but also the whole fourteen days for $200 per day. I didn't agree, but said nothing and wrote another disbursing order. Then of course, because the client got his way he became nice to me and apologized for his behavior, while his partner glared at me. I told him to forget it because I understood that he was under terrible stress, which was probably true. He calmed down, and asked me out for a drink after work, and he told the supervisor what a wonderful, patient person I was. Excuse me, but he was still a dreadful man. I shook his hand and he and his partner left with $2800. It was very hard for me, but I had to be flexible and accept the supervisory decision, but I sure didn't have to go out with the jerk.

The woman finally came downstairs with an adorable little child. She was young, an exotic beauty with jet-black hair and a gorgeous creamy latte complexion. I looked at the little toddler running around, and realized he would never know his father or have any idea what had happened, or why his mother was near collapse. Henry told us to leave and he would stay behind with the other supervisor and work with the woman. The image of the woman and her child imprinted on my mind. It was so sad and I felt so sorry for them, but there was nothing I could do to make it better. I felt helpless and overwhelmed.

So, we left for the evening. Six of us walked through the Red Zone and past the checkpoints, dodging traffic and obstacles on the way to the subway. By the time we got back to Brooklyn, it was dark and we were tired and extremely cold. I was too exhausted to take the Metro back to the hotel. I just couldn't face all of the stairs, so I hung around the Chapter, and took the bus back at 8:15 p.m. It took until 9:50 p.m. to get to Park Central. The bus driver seemed to understand how tired we were. The people on the bus were having a good time, but the outreach workers never said a word. Between us was sadness like a cloak wrapping around our tired bodies and minds. We were exhausted with glassed-over eyes, anxious to go to bed in spite of knowing it would be a series of nightmares when we finally got there. We had acquired the thousand mile stare.

The driver did tell us an interesting fact. There were three main bridges out of Manhattan and the way to remember their names was to think of BMW: Brooklyn, Manhattan, and Williamsburg. I think that was all I heard as he rattled on more stories and jokes. When we got back to the hotel and I returned to my room, I looked in the mirror and saw an image that looked like a stranger. I had lost weight, had gray bags under my eyes and I reeked of death. I went straight to bed, not even taking a shower or eating dinner. I was exhausted.

7 October 2001 – Sunday
Ground Zero, New York

Today we returned to the same building in the Red Zone next to the "pile". A Red Cross worker, an elderly woman from Missouri said she had been to fifteen National disasters in Family Services function, but she had absolutely no clue how to interview, or do the paperwork. I had to train her, and it was nearly impossible, but I was gentle and patient. To all appearances she was suffering from memory loss. The supervisor finally realized she wasn't going to learn, and put her at the reception desk. He was kind to her and made certain that she still felt useful. Disaster responses weren't a place for a person who couldn't take care of him or herself. I felt it was a safety issue, especially with someone like her.

The supervisor sent a local volunteer to my card table for me to train. I was to teach him the paperwork and get him started. He was a pleasant man in his thirties, or early forties, with a gentle manner and a heavy Greek accent. I instructed him to observe, as I interviewed a tall, thin dark-haired woman from the neighborhood, who twisted her hair, arms, and legs, constantly twitching as she spoke. She sank so far into the folding chair that she almost became part of it. I gave her a hug and a teddy bear before I began to interview her. The man watched intently. The woman was on Broadway Street the morning of September 11, and had witnessed the entire event. She had seen bodies jumping and falling from the horror of the upper floors of the towers, and as she told me her story she looked at me with a vacant stare. She had run for her life when the Towers collapsed, losing her shoes on the street, and badly cutting her feet. We talked as I filled out forms and disbursing orders. She told me she could no longer concentrate on anything, or sleep without terrible nightmares. I listened sympathetically and gave a high sign to the mental health worker, who came over and sat with us. After I finished the paperwork, the mental health worker took the woman to a secluded corner where she spent more than an hour attempting to defuse some of my client's stress. Our mental health team had gotten smaller and smaller. Many had left. I think they had more sense than I did. I was always thinking there would be just one more person I could help without thinking about my own well-being. I understood that I could easily be replaced, but I just couldn't leave when I knew there were more families to assist.

The Greek volunteer was soft-spoken, and highly intelligent. I brought another case to the table and let him handle it. He went through the process without a flaw. His clean hands paged through his notes with meticulous manicured nails. Who was he? After his client was gone, I asked him what he did for a living. He looked me in the eye and told me he was in the medical profession and asked me not to draw anyone's attention to that fact. He was giving his weekend to the Red Cross, a super man and a definite asset to our team. With the doctor, we now had eleven workers at the site. The Greek doctor worked on his own, like an experienced caseworker, never asking me any questions, and never making an error in his work. He handled clients with the utmost respect and compassion. Occasionally, he would glance over to my table and give me a wink.

My next client was an older blonde woman dressed in expensive clothing with an abundance of gold jewelry adorning her neck and wrists. She was so nervous that she would forget her English and lace her conversation with a dose of Russian. She and her husband were investors, and ran their business out of their apartment, which was not uncommon for the area. A week previous to the attacks they had canceled all their insurance in order to have more monies available for their business. That morning the dust was like a dark wall destroying all their dreams, equipment, and plans for the future; it left them penniless. My supervisor was sitting with me watching how I handled her and the paperwork. I pretended he wasn't there and poured my energy into the woman. I gave her financial assistance and several referrals to other agencies that might be of some help to her. She lingered, telling me her story. Finally she thanked me, took my hand and kissed it, then as quickly as she had appeared at my table, she was gone.

The supervisor told me I was doing a great job. The supervisors on the job were good to me. My entry level position in Red Cross was that of a technician. I enjoyed the work, but I wanted more responsibility. The supervisors spent time with me, and were critical of my work, so I could learn and move forward to the next level, which was that of a specialist.

As my client walked out of the door our nurse asked me and another caseworker to go upstairs to visit a woman, who was only in her apartment for the allotted four hours. As a caseworker, I would be able to open a case, if necessary and get the woman benefits to start her on the road to recovery. I hadn't done many home visits, and was anxious for the experience, so I was grateful for the opportunity.

The dirt and dust clung to hospital green walls inside the building complimenting the smell of mold exuding from the elevator. We rode to the fourth floor and stepped out onto the wall-to-wall dull red flowered carpeting of the 50's era that lined the long, narrow, dark green halls. It looked like an inexpensive hotel, and of course everything was at its worst from the attack. The EPA had placed machines in the halls, which looked like little microphones on skinny stands that made quick gasping noises as if they too were struggling for air. They were every ten feet making an attempt to get readings on the safety level of the environment.

We entered a nice apartment that was in disarray. An older woman lived there, who was apparently quite spoiled. She wanted a Jacuzzi for her tub when she moved back in because she had so much stress that she claimed it had damaged her body. We visited and told her she would have to get a certificate from her doctor stating her needs, and then get back to us. It was amazing how self-centered the woman was thinking only of herself when all around her people were in need and suffering.

When we returned to the lobby, I finished up my day working with a family, who were having great difficulty with their smaller children. They told us that overnight the children had entirely changed. They were afraid of everything, and every noise. I sat and read to their little girl, while her parents consulted with our mental heath staff. The child was only about four, and very sweet. She tenaciously clung to me, as she had to her mother. Even the little girl had her story to tell, as I listened to how she had seen "people fly" from the Towers. She pulled her brown braid into her mouth and sucked on the pink ribbon attached to it. Tears trickled down her face and across her flushed cheeks, as she asked me if the bad man was going to come to her apartment. It broke a piece of my heart to realize what the children had seen, and how frightened they were. I gently kissed her forehead, wiped away her tiny tears, and told her everything would be fine and not to worry. As I continued to read to her, her eyes grew heavy, and she fell asleep on my lap, innocently trusting that I had told her the truth.

8 October 2001 – Monday
Ground Zero, New York

In the morning, I passed through the barricades and walked with my team in the bitter, cold winds to Battery Park. When we arrived at the building where we were going to set up an office, a Red Cross emergency response vehicle (ERV) was there unloading supplies. Everything had changed. The security had intensified, if that was possible. The previous night Red Cross had told us that none of our vehicles would be allowed past the checkpoints, yet the ERV was there. The ERV that came in didn't belong and its team was relieved of their duties and sent home. The soldiers escorted them out of the Zone. Another ERV parked in front of the Marriott was stuck in the Zone. Why had the security tightened? Perhaps it was because of the rumor about the authorities bringing out a Brinks truck full of gold bullion from the "pile". I didn't know. I often wondered how we got into the Zone considering Red Cross didn't do background checks on their workers.

So began my day. I was doing continuous casework. I no longer went across to the bathroom without a mask. We all cut back on our water because the toilet facilities were so ghastly that we dreaded going there. There was so much stuff in the air that it was almost visible. All the workmen were wearing masks, and so was I. The previous night when I went back to the hotel, my lungs felt like someone was sitting on my chest. The cough had gotten worse and my lungs sounded like the rattle of chains.

Around ten o'clock a well-dressed woman in her fifties came in. I looked at her, and thought how nice it would be to take a long bubble bath, put on clean clothing, and go out to a classy bar and have a Manhattan, or two, or three. I needed a haircut, and some nice clothes. Even though I got a shower every day, I think the dirt on my clothing and my hair, along with my uniformed appearance was getting to me. Well, it was a good thought, but I put it aside and went back to work.

Business was slow, so around eleven o'clock, I went to the Marriott for lunch, but they had run out of food. I thought that having some time, I would walk out past the checkpoint in search of some exercise and lunch. A large contingency of uniformed airplane personnel was being escorted in by the police to pay their respects to their deceased colleagues. They were all dressed in blue airline uniform suits and had their hats tucked neatly under their arms. They were absolutely silent, as they moved in two lines toward the "pile", a solemn parade. It was so sad, and I wondered where we all got the courage to even be working in either Zone, let alone those pilots going back to work flying passenger planes in such bad times. None of us knew what was going to happen within even the next hour. We worked hard but always the thought in the back of our minds was that we could die here. I stood there and watched the airplane personnel and it photographed into my nightmares and moved in slow motion. I quickly left.

I turned my attention back to exiting the Red Zone thinking again of buying lunch. I walked past two men in full blue body suits, who were hosing down cars that were leaving the Zone. All I could see was their eyes. They were holding large hoses. I wondered what I carried on my shoes. I passed through the side of the fencing and stepped into the outside world of the Yellow Zone where I found an Italian deli. The proprietor was from Naples, and told me the Asians were pushing them out of the neighborhood. I could sense trouble there. I bought an Italian salami sandwich, which was delicious, and thought what a stranger I was in New York only being familiar with her present problem, and having no idea what transpired in the neighborhoods on a normal basis.

After lunch, I hurried back to see the building manager speaking with two of the supervisors. He was shaking his fist and shouting that he wanted us out of the building. He was very loud, but in a strange way I knew he wasn't angry. The well-dressed short, chunky man had an unlit cigar in this mouth that waved with every word he spoke. He said our presence reminded the tenants about what happened. Like get a grip – look outside! You couldn't even go out the door without a mask. Everywhere you ran into cleaning equipment, noise, workmen, police, fire, rescue personnel, the military, and helicopters flying right over us, destruction and debris, what felt like constant tiny earthquakes as huge trucks lumbered by, and to top all of that off the slight smell of death. Tenants had broken their leases and had already left, which created terrible stress for managers and owners of the local properties. It wasn't just tenants that were suffering from the economic impact of the attack.

As I was working, my cell phone rang and for once I didn't disconnect the caller. It was radio KSRO in Northern California calling to speak to me about doing an interview that my Chapter had arranged. I agreed to call them the next day during broadcast time. The public wanted to know what was going on at Ground Zero, and the media didn't have the access I did.

After four more clients, our day was done and we trudged out of the Red Zone, caught the Metro and returned to Brooklyn. As we finished up at headquarters, I decided to take the subway back to the hotel. I was really tired and hoped to get to bed earlier than if I had taken the bus.

At headquarters, I met Erma, a dumpy woman, who was a mental health worker from Oregon. She was going to my hotel, Park Central and wanted to ride with me. We went to the Metro where we caught the "A" train and got off at 59th Street. I wasn't sure what was up with the mental health staff, but they always seemed to hang out with the Ground Zero workers. I guess they couldn't understand how we held up. To understand the Red Zone you had to work there and there was no way I was going to talk about it when I got out of there each day.

When the train stopped there was quite a crowd. The mob pushed us into separate groups, and I went up the wrong stairs, but eventually corrected myself and caught up with Erma. On the way to the hotel in midtown Manhattan, we walked past an Italian restaurant called Joe G's. It was down a flight of stairs below street level. There was a personable young Puerto Rican man outside who was trying to bring in customers. He spotted my work jacket and stopped us, asking questions about Red Cross. As we spoke, he pointed to a menu display, which intrigued me as I read the interesting combinations of Sicilian foods offered. He invited us to come down and see the restaurant. My companion, Erma, whispered in my ear, "You can't go down there by yourself. It might not be safe." Safe, what did she know about being safe? I didn't understand her attitude. Erma saw I was going down the steep stairs to investigate, so she quickly left. I entered the establishment through a heavy wooden door with a beveled glass window on the upper section etched with a map of Sicily. As I pushed it open I found a narrow, charming restaurant with a lovely old bar hugging one wall. A rectangular-shaped glass mirror ran behind the bar, reflecting a variety of alcoholic beverages, and Italian liqueurs in their different shaped colored bottles. There were tables on the opposite wall and, in the rear, intimate little booths with red candles sitting on cloth covered tables, surrounded by old-fashioned wooden chairs. The softness of the oak paneled walls added to its quiet ambience. The restaurant cried out for me to stay, and to bury myself in good food and a cold beer. I spoke to the owner briefly, and then left, returning to the hotel where I changed my clothes into something less identifiable, and went back for dinner. The old Sicilian owner was happy to see me as he spoke to me in Italian and I replied in my broken Italian.

I sat at a little table next to an older man who was an exchange teacher from Italy. He was teaching chemistry at a New York public school. I had a good meal of pasta with meat sauce, a small pizza, San Francisco-type sourdough garlic bread, Pedroni Italian beer, and Parmesan cheese with Greek olives. It was delicious and relaxing reminding me of home. I enjoyed particularly the Sicilian pizza with my beer and the conversation with the teacher. The restaurant was a perfect place to relax with its subdued lighting and friendly atmosphere. The owner insisted on paying for my beer. He loved the work the Red Cross was doing in his city, and he treated me like royalty. When the public responded to Red Cross in that fashion, it made my job easier and gave me more incentive to continue, even when I was exhausted. That basement Italian restaurant became my own private respite. The waiters knew I was a Ground Zero worker and always gave me an after dinner drink gratis. Normally, I spoke to no one. The staff totally respected my need for privacy and solitude in the back of the restaurant where I usually sat. I went there at any opportunity I got after work, even if it was late. I needed to regroup and had found the perfect place.

I walked back to the hotel satisfied from the good meal and ready to sleep. In the morning I had to face the KSRO radio interview, and I needed some rest. It was going to be my day off finally, so my friend Patti and I planned to spend our time at the Metropolitan Museum of Art. We were going to go right after the radio interview.

9 October 2001 – Tuesday
Manhattan, New York

Last night was the first time since arriving in New York that I slept all night. I got up early, wrote some cards, and took a long walk in the rain to find a store to drop off my film. I was shocked to hear the news that we had bombed Afghanistan – more people killed. I guess I wasn't that shocked because I was expecting some sort of retaliation, but truly didn't understand considering that the terrorists on the planes were all from Saudi Arabia. I visualized more souls marching into the rubble of the World Trade Center. An odious act of terrorism would claim how many more lives?

I met Patti at eight o'clock as planned, and told her we couldn't leave till ten because I had to do the radio interview. She said she looked for me yesterday because she won three $3,000 tickets to Carnegie Hall, and wanted me to go with her. She sat in front of ex-president Clinton to see Bill Cosby. I couldn't have gone because I was out in the field and got in too late. She took two of her coworkers and they had a wonderful time. I wondered what she wore. She was working in headquarters, so she didn't have to cope with the dirt and smell.

The radio interview was only about fifteen minutes in length, but it made me nervous. I was vague and cautious in replying to every question asked. There was so much about the job that was not public news. They basically wanted to know what my role was, and what Ground Zero was like. I just told them exactly what I was doing and nothing more.

I met Patti in the hotel lobby as soon as the interview was over, and we took off for the museum. The hotel was on 55th Street and 7th. Avenue and we cut over to 5th Avenue. When we got to 50th Street and 5th Avenue there were a dozen fire engines, squad cars, and detectives. No matter how we tried to escape the stress, it was all over us. I took some pictures and we walked by not wanting to know what was wrong. We walked all the way to 88th Street. The blocks were short, but still a long walk. It gave us time to look around at the beautiful statuary and buildings of the city. Central Park was like stepping into the country; even the city's pulse slowed there, but it was windy and cold. Two blocks before the museum a vendor's cry echoed in the wind. There was an abundance of them selling photos of New York, souvenir clothing, and food. I bought a photo of the World Trade Center to take home, so my friends and family could see how beautiful it once was.

We arrived at the museum in about an hour, and were surprised to find it took up a couple of blocks. We climbed enormous stairs to the entrance of the Gothic-Revival-style building. There was a security guard who took our bags and searched them. I didn't think I would ever get used to having my things gone through. I asked what the entrance fee was and they said a donation but not so. In order to enter the exhibits you had to pay $10 for a tag, which let you anywhere in the museum. The clerk saw my Red Cross sweatshirt and gave me a ticket for $5.00.

Patti was from Tennessee, and was a Family Services Specialist. She was in good physical shape and had a quick wit. I enjoyed her company. We spent about three hours basking in the visual beauty of art. The museum was good for me because it didn't have any unpleasant odors, and I got to see paintings that I studied while attending the university. We saw the works of Rembrandt, Vermeer, Joshua Reynolds, John Constable, Gainsborough, Picasso, and many more. The sorrows of Ground Zero couldn't penetrate the walls of the museum. It was a temporary break for us. We were both very tired, but had so much stress to burn that we walked for hours. I became totally engrossed in the beauty all around me; instead of the ugliness I had been living with and seeing daily.

We stopped at the museum café for lunch before leaving. As we ate an interesting oriental chicken dish, we discussed the art and how Patti's grandmother had been a painter and done very well for herself in the market place. On our way out we stopped at the gift shop, but it was too expensive to even buy a bookmark.

As we strolled down the street, Patti bought me an ice cream from a vendor, and we meandered toward the park, licking away at our sweet treasures like two little kids.

We decided to walk through Central Park, not caring in the least if we got lost. It was an attractive, clean place with beautiful vegetation. The diversity in the city was marvelous. We walked by an Asian bride in a Western style white gown, the groom in a black tuxedo, and the four bride's maids in long red satin dresses giggling and following behind like a small flock of colorful birds. A professional photographer was with the group angling for a good picture, snapping one picture after another. We passed a gay dog walker who had ten excited charges leaping and jumping about. He was a puppet master manipulating the leashes with incredible grace; not one of the dogs got tangled up. We passed nannies pushing strollers with little children bundled up in heavy clothing with only their tiny faces peeking out, enjoying a ride in the cold air. We saw another bride and groom with their photographer posing them by a lake. The bride's white dress spread out in billows of satin over the grass, as the groom stood behind her with a nervous expression on his face. There was a dark-skinned, homeless man sitting on a bench under a sycamore tree singing sea shanties and two lovers embracing by another picture-perfect lake. We walked quite a ways, coming out on 86th Street. Once out of the park the world of terror became a reality again, with the screaming sirens of police cars roaring past. It was a long walk back to 55th Street and 7th Avenue, but it was liberating. Patti and I went to Joe G's for an early dinner to top off our easygoing day and rest our sore feet.

10 October 2001 – Wednesday
Ground Zero, New York

There was an enormous parade in Manhattan, and Mayor Giuliani encouraged New Yorkers to try to get their lives back to normal, to be strong, and to attend public functions. I prayed the parade would be safe.

I knew this would be the day I got a new job, and I did. We were late getting into the Chapter in Brooklyn because the traffic was congested. The police were randomly stopping cars and questioning people, which snarled everything up. There were multitudes of soldiers and police on the streets, and security seemed even tighter than usual.

When I arrived at headquarters, I went directly to the staff meeting. I had had a day off and I knew that there would be changes, and I was right. They were splitting up our team and reassigning us. There were no reasons given, but I suspected it was tightened security. I hung around for hours waiting for an assignment. I wandered throughout headquarters checking back in every half-hour at the Family Service office to see where I was to go. After a couple of hours, I decided just to sit and read the paper and wait. My friend and coworker, Stephanie, was sitting by the window patiently reading a book, waiting also. Finally, the clerk called our names. Stephanie and I were to report immediately to a service center one block outside of the Red Zone in the Yellow Zone still south of Canal Street with the same rotten air.

I was delighted that I would still be working with Stephanie, who was a local volunteer who lived in New York City. She had been on the outreach team with me. She was a humanitarian and a terrific worker, who operated a soup kitchen that catered to elderly people in Manhattan, so she had a good sense of how to handle our clients. When we had breaks, we would have long conversations about humanitarianism. The attack on New York had a staggering affect on Stephanie's world. She was putting in long hours with Red Cross to assist the city toward recovery.

On the corner of Harrison and Hudson Streets was the building we were to report to, an old union hall temporarily converted to a Red Cross service center. Stephanie and I entered a large, stifling room that looked like it had been in normal times a library and office, with two doors, one on each side of the room, and a dozen windows. It was the entire first level of the building. I figured divided it would make about five offices but it was open space, just one very large room. We greeted a young English woman at the reception table, and descended a steep flight of stairs into an incredibly noisy basement. We noticed that there were no windows and the air was stale, but still better than the air on the streets. The only other exit was at the other end of the basement office, a narrow staircase with white brick walls. It was indeed an old building. There was an elevator but no one seemed to use it. Family Service workers were individually conducting interviews, while other clients sat in a waiting area, either sleeping or eating the abundance of Red Cross snack food. In one corner was an office area for Records and Reports. They had dozens of cardboard boxes full of case files lined up on three tables. The coordinator and the supervisors' desks were sandwiched between Records & Reports and the mental health workers' area. In the rear behind a curtain was a room for the nurses. There were two large floor fans at each end of the long room, but they didn't do much to relieve the stuffiness. They only added to the stress with their loud screeching sound as their blades beat into the air and rubbed along the fan guards. The office had a series of fourteen rectangular folding tables, two rows of seven, with chairs for the caseworkers and the clients. There were too many people in the basement office, and I was sure that under normal circumstances the fire department would not have allowed it. I felt many things were being overlooked, because the entire city's focus was on Ground Zero and with so many dead from police and fire departments not much could be inspected.

A Red Cross supervisor took us into a dimly-lit, good-sized storage closet with a light hanging down on an electrical wire where he gave us a brief rundown on what we would be doing. We knew the work, but they wanted us to sit with another caseworker until they were sure we understood. That didn't last because we ended up helping the supposed trainer with her paperwork, which immediately put us out on our own.

I called out a client's name and an elderly woman of medium height, her body hidden beneath a black woolen coat, stepped forward from the waiting area. I greeted her with a warm smile and led her to my worktable where she sat clutching a large brown envelope. I asked her what we could do for her, and she slowly opened her old black leather purse and withdrew granny glasses with gold frames that flattered her dark chocolate skin. She placed them carefully on her face. As they slipped down onto the lower part of her broad nose, she withdrew a pay receipt from the envelope and handed it to me. It was a hotel in Brooklyn. Her place of employment in the Trade Center having been destroyed the main office in Brooklyn gave her the pay receipt. I opened the case and excused myself, telling her that I would have to make a phone call to verify her employment. When I was on the phone Steph came over and said that I had better return to my table because the client wanted to speak to me. The woman told me she lied and that she didn't work at the Trade Center, but was desperate for assistance because she was supporting her parents and her niece, and had depleted all her financial resources. I told her she didn't qualify under the program. As I searched my reference book for names and telephone numbers of places she could go for assistance, she silently got up and left. I called out to her, but she ignored me and quickly walked out the door back onto the New York streets. I felt terrible that her situation had forced her to come to us and lie. She was just another American who had fallen through the cracks driven by poverty and desperation, trying to survive.

All day I sat and listened to clients who were going over the edge with fear because of the recent events. The stress level moved up several notches, making my job more difficult. I was good at the casework and enjoyed it tremendously despite the intensified conditions. The coordinator wanted me to train the other technicians in the paperwork, especially the case forms. I thought so fast that I expected other people to respond with equivalent speed, and they often didn't, so I always had to exercise concentrated patience.

Starting tomorrow we would be working the a.m. shift (5:45 a.m. to 3:45 p.m.). I liked the hours because I would get back to the hotel before dark, but, knowing Red Cross, there was seldom a day as short as ten hours, and I knew things would change. Steph showed me how to return to the hotel on the subway from our new location. I was getting used to how all that worked and was enjoying my independence.

I was running out of money, and decided to use my VISA and reimburse myself when the Red Cross staff reimbursement and travel expense check arrived. Meals in New York were expensive. Our usual daily allotment was $30, but in New York City it was $40. The money was for our meals, having laundry done, and tips for the maids at the hotel. We only claimed what we used. In some places in the USA, we never even needed the $30. Given $500 when assigned to a job, when we got down to $200 it was necessary to put in a request for more money, but I had not done that. I had let it run considerably lower, but wasn't really concerned having my VISA card with me.

At the Chapter in Brooklyn the Red Cross kept giving us things. They sent a box to the service center full of items we might need. I received a new red shirt, a purple Red Cross sweatshirt, and a cap with a New Jersey logo on the bill. I think they were trying to make our job a little easier.

I arrived at the hotel after work, tired and in need of personal space. Working in the service center, I left my disbursing orders there at night, so the trip to Brooklyn was no longer required, and that made it possible for me to get to the hotel earlier. The service center had its own Records and Reports office, which made it so much easier for all of us.

After I changed, I decided to take a walk to alleviate the stress from all the stories I had heard during the day. As I left the hotel, I bumped into Patti coming home from work. She asked me if she could go with me, so we walked farther down Times Square. She was looking for a drug store and a new pair of shoes. We found the drug store, but she didn't find the shoes. We walked down 7th Avenue past splashy animated giant signs advertising youth and beauty, past buildings housing renowned Broadway shows, restaurants, and the famous wax museum on 8th Avenue. It was awesome! New York was so alive; it just absorbed my mind and body. I had fallen in love with the city.

We stopped at Engine 54, Ladder 4, Battalion 9, on 8th Avenue. The entire front of the firehouse was an array of flowers, red carnations, white and yellow daisies, pink roses, colorful variegated bunches still in florist wrap. Placed along the brick ledge outside were different size candles. There was a tall unlit votive candle with a picture of Saint Anthony on the front, and two small Canadian flags sticking out of the top. Taped to the walls were children's drawings depicting the Towers burning, fire trucks, and American flags. There also were cards from adults, as well as children, from all over the country offering prayers and encouragement to the survivors. In a prominent place by the firehouse door was a framed picture with photos of fifteen firemen, five across and three down, much like placement in a yearbook. The frame was thin and black and the photographs were in color. They were headshots of the uniformed men in happier times, posed in front of a fire engine. Above the picture were the words, "Our Brothers". Below the picture on a podium was a condolence book, which we signed. We felt deep emotion for their suffering. To the side of the firehouse stood a life-sized Statue of Liberty covered with so many small American flags and cards, that we could only see the torch and the green face of the Lady. People milled around in silence with a terrible sadness in their eyes. Two firemen stood like sentinels guarding the picture of their dead. I had heard and seen so much that my emotions were numb. I didn't know if I wanted to spend an hour in church praying, or get a bottle of wine and just cry. I was exhausted when we returned to the hotel and too tired to eat dinner. I showered and went to bed. I had to take a sleeping pill because it kept the nightmares at bay, and I needed as much sleep as possible in order to be able to handle the clients fairly.

11 October Thursday
Manhattan, New York

Today started badly. The supervisor on the new job told me to meet her at 5:00 a.m. in the lobby. In the meantime, another worker said they were all leaving at 4:45 a.m., and if I wasn't there I would be left behind. I arrived at 4:45 a.m. and went with a group of six Red Cross workers to the café across the street, where they apparently ate breakfast every morning. At about 5:10 a.m. along came the supervisor, furious because she had waited for me, and I had gone. Great start with a new boss! After breakfast, they all paraded to the subway like a row of ducklings. I would have preferred to travel alone, or with a buddy, but I had to learn the way, so I followed.

The air had the smell of death in it as we surfaced from the Metro. The smoke had increased and the cold weather pressed the bad air downward capturing it for the day over Ground Zero, adding to the gloom. I hoped I would escape it in the basement, but not so. Added to the closeness and stuffiness of the office, my eyes still burned and my clothes still had that ever present faint odor of death.

There was supposed to be a staff meeting, which eventually happened, but was late. We learned that the plumbing system in the building was giving out. A nurse announced that we needed to drink more water, but in the same breath she told us to limit our use of the toilets. There was one functioning toilet on the third floor, and if that gave out they would close down the service center. That left no facilities available for our clients.

Also, the officer told us to make sure and have the supervisors sign all the disbursing orders before we gave them to the clients. That meant that the worker and the clients would have to wait. I was sure there was a better way to expedite the procedure. The present coordinator seemed to be more concerned that the boxes on the forms were correct, than what was happening to the clients.

Stephanie and I worked the first case together. The clients were a middle-aged Chinese couple who lived and worked south of Canal Street. They had limited English skills, so I requested one of the translators be available for the case. They were local volunteers and invaluable to us while dealing with the population of Chinatown. Without them we would not have been able to assist the non-English speakers. Our boundary South of Canal Street divided Chinatown in half causing many problems because the people clearly didn't understand why the entire neighborhood wasn't eligible to receive aid.

One particular couple who were clients had nine people living in their apartment. We worked with them for about an hour attempting to sort out their needs. The interpreter was a soft-spoken, patient woman who was Chinese-American and a teacher at a local college. She was pleasant and understanding, making our job simpler and putting the clients more at ease. Before we were done, the Chinese couple's relatives were sitting on the chairs lined up against the brick wall of the basement waiting for service. We had to explain to them that everyone listed on their form as family could not reapply for duplicate benefits. I wasn't sure if they understood or not, but hoped they did.

As the morning continued, the noise level increased and the room grew hotter, making everyone sleepy. Stress covered the office like a shroud, creating short tempers, impatient clients, and weary caseworkers. I would stand and wait and wait to see the overworked supervisor, while my client would sit and wait. The only positive side of the delay was that I used the time lapse for mental health to speak with my clients. Most all the clients had mental health issues because they were still in shock, and functioned under a cover of fear on a daily basis. It was a difficult time for all of us, but the interpreters were fabulous assisting everyone they could.

It was one month since the attack and the people were emotional wrecks. We had brought them into a hot, oppressive, loud environment, which wasn't much help to their nerves, but what choice did we have? Where were we going to get facilities that could deal with that many people? A guitarist showed up and played for a few hours, but the poor man really did nothing but add to the stress and noise level. There had to be another way. It was frustrating because I could have processed clients so much faster, even still taking time to talk to them. It was like being in high school. I got a break at 11:30 a.m. and Steph and I took lunch.

We went to a fancy bakery in a building with a brick façade. It must have been an old factory converted into the present day bakery. Steph bought soup and a salad, but I didn't eat because I was getting low on funds and wasn't very hungry anyway. I wanted to eat a good dinner and looked forward to relaxing in the Italian restaurant around the corner from the hotel that evening. After lunch we took a walk in the sun and the smell. Working in the basement we lacked exposure to daylight and were willing to put up with the putrid odors, just to get outside. If we didn't get out during the day we would never have seen the light. The smoke seemed to be getting worse, as the weather deteriorated, and it got closer to winter. It pressed down like an anvil hammering the neighborhood and reminding them that things were not all right. After about a half an hour we went back to work. It was tedious and each case was slow. All of our clients were from Chinatown, and most required interpreters. Their lack of language skills cut the communications between them and our mental health workers considerably.

We got off work shortly after 3:00 p.m. and I knew my way back to the hotel, so I decided to travel on my own. I needed the space. After being under such pressure all day, I began to covet my time alone. I could walk down through Times Square among thousands and be totally by myself because of my anonymity, but my fellow workers continually asked me to the Broadway shows and Carnegie Hall. I knew everyone had their own way to process stress, but didn't they mourn for our people? Or, maybe that was how they handled it. Our job was difficult, and party time made no sense to me. There were 3,000 people buried and burned several blocks from our service center. I needed quiet and space to attempt to process what had happened. The complexity of the job was draining my spirit. I knew I would never look at life the same after I left New York City.

I did make it to the Italian restaurant for supper. The staff was friendly, and they left me alone. They knew who I was and where I had been working. I worked on my journal over a beer with a plate of cheese and olives. I usually ordered pasta, and when I was finally ready to leave, the staff gave me an after dinner-drink. They were nice to me, packing me a small bag of snacks to take to work the next day and never charged me for them.

After dinner, I walked down to Times Square and back over to the firehouse – Engine 54 on 8th Avenue to photograph the memorial. I asked the handsome fireman in front for permission to take pictures, and he thanked me for my courtesy. It was so sad there. I took a roll of film of the unique scene. The firemen had put up a sign on the front of the building above the memorial with the words, "Engine 54, Ladder 4, Battalion 9, FDNY Wants to Thank Everyone for their Support." The firemen standing in the doorway watched the onlookers with soulful eyes, as if expecting to see their lost "brothers" appear in the crowd.

I walked around Times Square taking pictures of the people of New York. I photographed beggars, which were in abundance, clowns advertising restaurants and shows, merchants selling everything from sweaters to souvenirs, lovers walking hand in hand through the crowds to a Broadway show, or a local bar, some tourists, and even a person dressed like a spaceman. That part of Manhattan seemed very far away from Ground Zero.

I had seen a photo with the Statue of Liberty as a watermark and in the foreground were the rescue personnel working on the pile. I looked for the store that sold the photo because I wanted to take it back to my Chapter, but was unable to find it. There were hundreds of people on the streets, and they were all in a rush to go somewhere. It was interesting to walk among so many, and be so alone. My solitude didn't last as my new supervisor, Juanita, stopped me on the street. She was on her way to see the musical *Aida* and walked a ways with me questioning me about what I did at my Chapter. I just couldn't understand how people like her could go, go, go and never slow down and center themselves. Didn't they ever get tired?

12 October 2001 – Friday
Manhattan, New York

My wake up call was at 4:30 a.m. because our new working hours were from 6:30 a.m. till 6:00 p.m. Long working hours were normal for a Red Cross job, so it didn't surprise me in the least. Six of us met in the lobby and went across the street to the café, mumbling and grumbling about how early it was. I am a morning person, so it was okay with me. I ordered a small orange juice, which cost me $3.95; can you believe that? I didn't order a breakfast because I preferred to eat in my room in the mornings, mainly because I didn't like café food. After breakfast, we walked for five dark blocks to the subway. The underground was stifling, smelling of urine and filthy clothing. The benches along the cracked-tiled walls, as well as the wooden benches in the middle of the platform were beds for the homeless, who had found a warm place to go on a cold fall night. The subway had no toilets that I saw, thus the smell.

Buried deep in a tattered green army blanket was a man with only his unshaven face exposed. There was so much black stubble that it ran up into his hair like some wild creature looking for a place to escape. I wondered what his history was, and what had brought him to be the man he was, sitting on a bench in a New York subway soaked in his own urine. How did the people in the vast world of the subway come to be who they were? More homeless individuals were sleeping on the "A" train when we boarded. Some were sleeping sitting up with their chins resting on their chests rocking back and forth to the rhythm of the train, and the sound of the wheels clacking on the tracks. On the long side seats reserved for the elderly or disabled, several men were sleeping. One woman who didn't look a day over thirty had black matted hair sticking to her soiled face. As she conversed with herself in a loud, annoying tone, she would look at an unsuspecting person and tell them that they'd better find Jesus, or they'd burn in hell. A black man with torn blue jeans and a filthy red checkered shirt held onto a pole for balance, as he shouted throughout our entire ride about his abusive childhood, warning every one about a communist plot to take over America. I wondered if he had ever washed his dreadlocks, as they lay on his head like the hair of a matted poodle. I watched him, and I believed that he wasn't aware that anyone else was in the car. Some of those lost souls rode back and forth on the trains all night long, just to have a warm place to sleep. Occasionally, a sleeping homeless person would be jolted to reality as the activation of the doors' automatic voice would say, "Stand clear of the closing doors," at which time the person would stand up slowly and saunter to the doors just making it before they closed. The transit police didn't bother them and as the day went on more and more homeless people left the subways for the streets above only to return after dark the next day. The daily passengers on the train either read the paper, or listened to CD players ignoring the pandemonium and the people who to them were invisible.

I arrived at work at 6:30 a.m. just in time for the staff meeting. After the meeting, the long day began in our basement. I worked on the standard ten or twelve-foot brown collapsible table. I put a Styrofoam cup of chocolate candy kisses on my "desk" along with two teddy bears in preparation for upset clientele. We turned on the two big fans because of the lack of windows, but as the day went on it got hotter and hotter, and the caseworkers started to complain because they were getting sleepy. I guess I was lucky on that one because I liked the heat.

There were twelve chairs in three rows of four. They were in the front of the room where the clients waited. There were two rectangular brown tables along the wall in the waiting area that had open boxes of candy and snacks neatly stacked along with daily newspapers and magazines. The clients waited as they grazed on the treats and paged through the reading materials. Some of the children loaded their mouths dropping wrappers under the chairs. One little girl didn't like her choice of a snack, so she spit it out on the floor. At the end of the day the waiting area was a disaster in itself. One older Chinese man fell asleep and was snoring, as three little children laughed and pointed at him. A woman juggled an infant on her lap, as she tried to change his dirty diaper, which only added to the dreadful odor in the office. All of the chairs in the waiting area were full. Most people spoke in a tongue that was foreign to my ears, but there were some English speakers laced throughout the group.

I picked up a file and called out a name, feeling much like a clinic clerk. A woman jumped from her chair – a human jack-in-the-box. She was a petite Irish woman with her gray hair pulled back off her face by two large golden moon-shaped barrettes. The women was hyper and twitched as she spoke, dressed in a brightly colored embroidered blouse that clung to her thin freckled arms. White cat hair coated her straight black skirt that emitted a scent of cheap perfume. She had thick woven stockings of many colors that protruded from her black convent like shoes. Her assortment of jewelry was amazing: dyed black and green seeds hanging from her neck and ears.

She was a published novelist in her forties who had lived in Battery Park, Ground Zero. She was in need of housing, a grant, and most of all a person to listen to her story. She shared her apartment with a female partner, and they had lost everything, including their computer equipment. They needed separate housing because her partner was busy drowning her fear in booze. She told me that after the incident, her roommate had not stopped drinking, and all they did was argue. She taught at a local school and in the summer months often toured with her published work. The woman was at school when the attack occurred and was not able to return home. She bonded to me and talked nonstop for about twenty minutes, as she continually chewed on her fingernails. As she spit them out they catapulted into my Styrofoam candy cups. She told me that she believed the entire incident was a cosmic event foretold by Nostrodamus. She guaranteed me that the world was about to end. At that point, I began to believe that on this job I had met every type of human being known to man. I gave her all that I could both financially and emotionally. The woman was so nervous that I brought the mental health worker to sit at my table, while I got my paperwork approved by the supervisor. I just didn't want to leave the woman alone. She was not capable of sitting still, and I was afraid that she would get up and leave.

I got my disbursing orders approved and returned to the table to explain them to her. The mental health worker had left, and the woman was waiting for me drumming her fingers on the table. "This work will bring you good Karma, young lady. I appreciate the help", she said as she quickly stuffed the papers into her red and black hand-woven Guatemalan shoulder bag. She jumped out of the folding chair, and leaned toward me. I gave her a hug, and could feel her shaking. I wished her the best of luck, at which she pushed through the waiting clients, and disappeared out the door.

After my client left, the mental health worker came to my table and informed me that the supervisor, who had gotten angry with me the other morning, had to go home because her blood pressure was too high. John and Bob were the new supervisors, and they were hard on me because they knew I wanted the rank of Specialist. They caught even the tiniest errors, but had a great interest in the welfare of the clients, which made it easy for me to work with them.

The next client I assisted was a strange Buddhist monk, who was spotlessly clean, dressed in a long brown robe of a soft woolen fabric. He had a shaved head, granny glasses with gold frames, and a beautiful manicure on his long soft fingernails giving the appearance that he had never worked a day in his life. As he clutched his soft brown woolen cloth shoulder bag, he sat so straight in the chair that it was like he had a rod up his back. With him came a loud, overbearing Asian man much his senior. He was a self appointed translator, definitely not from our staff. Living north of Canal Street the monk wasn't eligible for any assistance through the disaster funds. I couldn't turn him away, so I tried to extract from him the reason for his sitting in front of me asking for assistance. He expressed a need for permanent housing. So, I spent over forty minutes patiently explaining that we did not provide permanent housing. I was going to give him a grocery voucher when the translator piped up that he lived in a temple with other monks, who provided his food, clothing, rent, and whatever he needed. So what was his point? He wanted to move because he didn't like the change in air quality in his neighborhood. I couldn't help him with anything, so I gave him phone numbers of other agencies. I also found out from making some phone calls that at Pier 94, another Red Cross location, there was a group of Buddhists who had an organization that assisted people like the monk. I told the translator and he relayed it to him. The monk had a fit, acting like a spoiled child. He didn't like the group and minced no words over the fact. I kept repeating myself with infinite patience, while the twelve chairs in the waiting area filled up with anxious people who wanted to speak with a worker. All of a sudden, he stood up, slowly pressed his brown robe with his hands, turned and left without another word. The translator quickly trotted off behind him out the door and up the stairs to dissolve into the rotten air.

At that I went to lunch with Steph. We went around the corner and walked down the cobblestone street. If it had not been for all the smoke, the old neighborhood with its brick buildings would have been quite charming. We went into the bakery/café and I had a problem trying to cash a $20 traveler's check. I had identification so they did decide to cash it, or they knew they weren't going to make a sale. I bought a skinny loaf of bread and Steph bought soup. We hid out in a cushioned booth in a quiet corner in the back of the bakery for fifteen minutes. Then we walked in the sun and smoke for another fifteen and then back to our basement world of clients and organized chaos.

After lunch, I opened a case with a particularly good looking Italian/American man, who had lost his business in the Trade Center. He had tears in his soft blue eyes and was struggling with the fact that he had to ask for assistance. He told me he had never asked anyone in his life for help, but his business was gone and all his employees were dead, and he didn't know where to turn. I needed to meet his emergency needs and give him referrals to other agencies. I told him the California lemonade story that I had invented, and he relaxed and even got a crack of a smile on his face.

California Lemonade Story

There were some little children in California who sold lemonade just for the people of New York who were suffering. They sent the money to the Red Cross to give to the people. (Then I would tell the proud client) "What do you want me to do, go back and tell those little kids you didn't want it?" (It got them every time.) They would smile through their pride and relax as I did my job.

He reached over and clutched my hand as he told me another story of death and destruction, and how he had been late to work, or he too would be dead. He said he was exhausted and felt so guilty that he hadn't died with the rest of his staff. As he spoke his hands began to sweat.

I paid the man's mortgage for the month, gave him a Family Maintenance Grant, a grocery voucher, a referral to the September 11 Fund and, of course, FEMA. I couldn't do much about his sorrow, except listen. He stared beyond me as he continued with his story, as if he was looking into the faces of the dead. I thought he might still be in shock, so I gave one of our mental health workers a high sign and he came over and sat with us. The man's thoughts were scattered as he also told us that he had heard the police were searching for the black boxes, but hadn't found them yet. Personally, I thought they must have disintegrated. Then he jumped to the subject of the recent anthrax that was turning up in the mail in Manhattan. It was like what next? I procrastinated processing his paperwork, so that the mental health professional would have more time to work with him. When I brought the papers back for his signature he had tears spilling down his cheeks. He left with the papers; his shoulders slumped over as he looked at the floor while walking toward the stairs.

We got off at 3:30 p.m. which was unbelievably early for Red Cross. Cymi, an amiable woman from my Chapter, Herbert from Guam, and another worker I hardly knew took the subway to 42nd Street. Cymi made sure that she took advantage of the entertainment New York had to offer. She stopped at the ticket office for the Lion King. Her plan was to go in the evening with friends and then out to dinner. She was unable to get the tickets because none were available for at least a month. She decided that we were all going to take a local tour on one of the red double-decker busses that we saw everyday around Manhattan. All Red Cross rode free courtesy of a loving and grateful New York. All that was required was we show our American Red Cross identification. We were welcomed aboard along with a dozen other tourists. We climbed a narrow spiral staircase to the top deck of the bus, where we sat in the cold for our tour. The guide was a plump short woman with a screechy voice. She perched herself on the front seat like an owl watching for prey never missing the opportunity to tell us every detail of our trip. The view was spectacular as we zipped in and out around midtown and uptown. I saw the Dakota Apartments constructed in 1884, where John Lennon was assassinated on December 8, 1980 and Rosemary's Baby was filmed. It was called the Dakota apartments because when it was built there was no city built around it and it was jokingly called the Dakota Territories. We passed the Metropolitan Opera House, and Central Park. We went through Harlem where Clinton had an office, and Spanish Harlem. As we did a loop and came around again to Central Park, I fell asleep. A tree branch on the edge of Central Park slapped my face and quickly revived me. I reached up and grabbed my Red Cross cap for fear of it flying off my head. I was embarrassed and hoped no one saw me sleeping. We got off at 59th Street and walked to 55th Street to the hotel. I changed my clothes and took off quickly for 46th Street to the store where I had finally found the photo poster of the incident. I wanted to bring it home and I wanted to be alone.

13 October 2001 – Saturday
Manhattan, New York

I got up at 4:30 a.m. for work. The ladies had the day off, so I met Herbert and John in the lobby at 5:30 a.m. We went up the street and had a bagel and then caught the subway. When we arrived at the service center, we had our usual staff meeting and then I went to work. With the almost daily changing rules, I had to be even more of an advocate for my clients. Every case I wrote was not just a narrative, but also a defense, a justification for what I was giving them.

My first clients of the day were a young couple with a tiny dog wrapped in a blue terrycloth bath towel. They sat before me with tears in their eyes clasping each other's hands as they spoke. The destruction of their Greenwich Street apartment was devastating. They lost their home and their jobs at a shop in the Winter Garden. Asbestos, fiberglass fibers, cement, bone dust, and toxic plastics covered the interior of their apartment. They were home at the time of the incident and escaped with only their dog, their lives, their cameras, and the clothing they were wearing. In their haste, the woman left without her shoes and had badly cut her feet, as they ran to the waterfront carrying their few belongings and the frightened dog.

The man hurriedly took photos before they left their apartment, which was smart because I had evidence of the damage and was able to get them furniture. The supervisor said no, but I begged so he sent me to the coordinator, who approved my request. The coordinator had a price list faxed to us from the Brooklyn Chapter. I had told the couple to return in the morning after I got things straightened out for them. I wanted time to get a price list, but before they left I had all the necessary information I needed. They were so grateful that they gave me two pictures of Ground Zero taken right outside of their apartment window. The area was a crime scene and they didn't know when they would be able to return home. In one morning the couple had lost everything except a little dog and a couple of cameras that were no longer in good condition.

My next client was the wife of a limousine driver. There was so much paperwork, which was so time consuming, but I got her substantial benefits. Her husband had rushed to China to see his dying mother, and she was representing him speaking impeccable English. The word came down that we could give benefits to the limo drivers, if they could prove with their trip tickets that most of their revenue came from around the Trade Center, and that there was a noticeable drop in their income after the attack. I sat with piles of trip tickets and my calculator trying to figure out his income before and after. The majority of his clients were from the Trade Center and there was a drastic reduction in his income. The woman was grateful for our assistance and thanked me as she left.

One of my coworkers was an older woman from upstate New York named Lois. She came over to my table after the Asian woman left. I don't know how it came up, but she asked if I would like to go with her to Mass after work. I think she saw the miraculous medal that I always wear and assumed that I was Catholic. Of course, I said yes.

When I got off of work, I rushed to the subway and returned to the hotel as quickly as possible. I cleaned up and hurried up the street to buy some deli food for dinner, and dropped it off back at my hotel room. I walked to 48th Street and 5th Avenue to St. Patrick's Cathedral. The church's gothic beauty was jammed between skyscrapers stunting its magnificence. It was a bastion of strength sitting like a barrier of faith next to the materialism of the fashionable stores where mannequins wore mink coats, and where outrageously expensive shoes were displayed in well lit store windows.

The streets were crowded with office employees leaving for various after work destinations, a sea of black clothing like an incoming tide heading non-stop for the subways. I met Lois on the stairs of St. Patrick's, and we entered the church going to the front to escape the tourists and the incessant flashing of their cameras. Minus only the frescos, the church was much like what I had seen in Europe, a haven in the middle of madness. I couldn't hide my emotions in church. The choir sang Amazing Grace with the accompaniment of a grand organ, and I cried. All the pressure of Ground Zero and all I'd seen and heard were too difficult for me to deal with in that environment. The images of the dead and missing flashed before me as they cried out to be discovered and returned to their families, the smell of rotting corpses, the rescue personnel, and each person that had come to me for assistance, but worst of all the children who were living with the trauma of evil and hate, the loss of their innocence as helicopters landed in their playgrounds, and as they witnessed humanity jump from the Towers. I prayed for strength, courage, and for peace. I felt better when I left the church, but not much. I glanced over at Lois and she too was crying. After Mass she said goodbye and went her way and I headed back to the hotel for dinner. I knew when I returned home, I would have to deal with my emotions. Right then it was important to be strong to best assist the clients. I so loved the people I was working with. They were unique, and had been through too much. They didn't deserve what happened to them and we didn't deserve it either. My work had become not only painful but very personal.

14 October 2001 – Sunday
Manhattan, New York

It was a heartbreaking day. I got into the basement early, which was good because I had time to munch on a bagel and get something hot to drink. Shortly after the staff meeting, I went upstairs to register new people. The old union hall building was dark and gloomy. Because the building sat on the corner we had two entrances, and our plan was to have the new clients enter on Harrison Street and the returning clients enter on Hudson Street. It was supposed to help avoid congestion, but the clientele was increasing by the hundreds, which was developing into a major problem.

I sat behind a rickety old card table in a small marble entrance way signing people up, so they could see a caseworker downstairs. Many were Asian and spoke no English, so it was necessary to radio for interpreters, which slowed everything down. They had to wait outside once registered because the fire department finally had checked our operation and decided we had too many people in the building. Once we brought them downstairs, they had to wait again for an available caseworker. A sizable and not clean local volunteer sat with me. She had stringy blonde hair, and stains down the front of her work vest. I showed her what to do, which wasn't much, just filing out registration cards, and directing the clients where to go. We couldn't even offer them toilet facilities because all but one on the third floor was out of order. The lack of toilets was threatening to close the service center down. People were losing patience, and the guard sitting across from us hid himself behind a marble counter and slept most of the morning. He didn't enhance our security system.

Near noon, a client downstairs had a convulsion and the nurses called an ambulance. The ambulance crew couldn't fit the stretcher bed into the archaic Otis elevator, and ended up carrying the patient out of the basement office in a chair. That added to the stress and tension among the clients, as well as the workers.

After that the supervisor pulled me off of the registration table and put me to work downstairs doing cases. They wanted the clients processed faster and couldn't spare a caseworker, so that was the end of my job upstairs.

My first client was another limo driver, who I assisted through mountains of paperwork. After he left, I took a registration slip, and went outside to call another client. My prospective client had chosen not to wait, so I stopped by the desk to pick up another slip when I saw a mental health worker standing on the sidewalk speaking to a potential client. The attractive victim was a forty-year-old, slender, well-groomed individual with platinum blonde wavy hair. Her face was red and swollen from crying and her mascara had run in black streaks down her cheeks. The worker turned to tell me that the woman was full of anger and had an unreasonable attitude. I didn't know what the worker wanted with me, but she told the woman I would help her. The client wasn't angry, just devastated and frightened. I took her into the front door, past all the waiting clients, down the stairs and to my table. I told her I had worked in the Red Zone and understood. I couldn't have understood the pain she was enduring, but I wanted to win her confidence. I wanted her to trust me and calm down, so I could be of assistance to her. She requested help and claimed she was desperate. I gave her a hug and told her there were quite a few things I could help her with. As we sat and talked she clutched the teddy bear I had given her as she began to tell her story.

She had come from Istanbul, Turkey some years ago and settled in New York. The woman loved the city and had in her words achieved the American dream of having a nice apartment and owning her own business. She lost her beauty salon and her apartment in the attack. I wrote her disbursing orders for which she was very grateful. She wanted to rebuild her salon, but over seventy of her clients were dead and she couldn't cope with that. As I explained to her that the funds the Red Cross was giving her were a gift from the American people, she wept. It was difficult to stay composed, but I did. She refused to talk to any of our mental health workers because of her first contact with the one upstairs. I was sorry because I thought she would have benefited from speaking to a qualified professional. I poured out love and compassion to her and it did help, but they could have done so much more. I felt drained after she left, but was not able to take a break because I had another client waiting for me.

It was another limo driver, who sat before me asking for help. I paid his car insurance and Con Edison bill. He was a soft-spoken intensely proud man who had made no money since September 11. We were not assisting all of the limo companies and it was causing problems. Drivers were coming to the center from Queens and the Bronx, many demanding the same benefits that their friends were receiving, who worked in and around the Trade Center. The drivers didn't understand why we paid some and not others, and often became livid. At times their anger was frightening because I couldn't read what was in their eyes as they glared at me. Often I would call over mental health and sometimes the supervisor also, and even as a team we couldn't defuse their anger.

When I went to get disbursing orders for the limo driver to sign, the supervisor who was going home pulled me aside and gave me a Metro pass, for which I was grateful because the passes were $17 for a weeks worth of rides. He said he didn't need it any longer and to please use it. When I had first arrived in New York the subways were free to Red Cross, but that ended and now we had to pay. I used the pass on the subway at the end of the day.

I finished processing the limo driver and the workday came to a welcome conclusion. After work, I didn't socialize. Many of the women from the service center were always out and I stayed away. I guessed that everyone had his or her own method of releasing tension. I was being plagued with nightmares and couldn't sleep more than four hours, unless I took a sleeping pill. My focus was on the clients and not myself, so it never occurred to me to go to mental health and talk to them about the nightmares. It was essential to be strong in front of the clients, so I was forcing myself to internalize my pain for their sake, and I was paying for it. My work performance was impeccable. I was not short-tempered or irritable and worked well with my group because I understood that there was a lot of pain for all of us. Mental health began to steer all the clients from Ground Zero to me. I was an advocate for my clients and I fought every issue to get more for them, and everyone I fought for took more out of me.

After work, I went right to the hotel where I changed my clothes and took off for Mass at St. Patrick's. My emotions were increasingly difficult to control when I got into church. It was just horror story after story all day long and I was so tired. I drew great strength from going to Mass and found the power of pray to be my total support.

After Mass, I walked for blocks to a business supply store where I found a folder for my poster and my photos, which was the wrong size. I would have to return it, but another day. I went back to the hotel dropped off my camera and package and walked down to the Italian restaurant, Joe G's. The streets had hundreds of people, who all seemed to be in a hurry racing off to different destinations in Manhattan. There was still a large police presence on the streets, and whenever a fire truck went by people would pause and look with admiration, as the large American flag standing on the back would whip and snap in the wind. Their heroes were still out there protecting them from unknown terror. I walked past a Hindu restaurant where two musicians sat with their backs to the window playing unfamiliar ragas on a sitar accompanied by a small silver drum, a Japanese restaurant with plastic samples of their dinners lining the window, and finally I arrived at Joe G's. As I entered the bartender, a beautiful dark-haired woman from Brazil who looked very Sicilian greeted me. I sat in the back and worked on my journal in the quiet by the light of a candle. The smells of delicious cooking wafted through the entire restaurant tempting my palate to eat more than I needed. It was so nice to smell something other than the fetid odors in the Zone. I spent a peaceful undisturbed hour lingering over my writing, my pasta and beer. When I paid my bill the waiter had packed a bag of garlic bread and Italian cookies for me, and with a smile said, "A snack for tomorrow. God take care of you guys out there."

15 October 2001 – Monday
Manhattan, New York

Today work was very crowded, and six Family Service workers were leaving. When I arrived at headquarters in Brooklyn in September, I signed papers saying if they needed me, I would extend my stay. I was skilled at what I was doing and there were so many to assist that I decided to continue my work. I would not have done that if I thought I couldn't handle it. Mental Health was watching me all the time because they couldn't understand how someone who worked at Ground Zero was still holding it together. I found a way to get to Mass every day after work, and that gave me the strength to pull me through. I put the entire thing in the hands of the Lord and prayed for the courage and strength to aid me in being as much use as possible to the people I was serving.

My friend Jane's emotions had reached a crisis level with the job in Records and Reports. She was young, tall, and had curly short auburn hair, very attractive, smart, and sweet. I liked her and had worked with her before on a job in Texas. She had signed up for two weeks, but was falling apart. All she did was read some of our cases and she was off talking to mental health, and I thought she should have considered leaving. As it was she cut her time down. It was no reflection on her because the job was a monster, but I wondered how she would have been in the field.

The press commended Red Cross for our policy of serving everyone equally. There was an issue with another agency denying the homosexual population benefits because they weren't recognizing them as family units. They were refusing to assist undocumented individuals who were also victims of the attack. It was difficult to believe that would come up as a problem, considering what the people were facing. It seemed so small to think like that. I was proud of the fact that I was part of a humanitarian organization that dealt with all the people. If they lived or worked south of Canal Street they received our services.

My supervisor directed a woman to my table, and told me that she lived one block from the Trade Center. I got up, introduced myself to the attractive dark-haired woman of forty-four, who looked not a day over thirty-five with her slender youthful figure, which was accented by black leather slacks and a multi-colored turtle neck sweater. I shook her perspiring hand and invited her to take a seat. She was anxious to tell me her story and expressed a need for assistance, as she took a chocolate candy kiss from the Styrofoam cup on my table. The woman was a single mother of two children, a girl of eight, and an older daughter, seventeen. She was a writer of children's books and worked in her apartment. Her use of the English language was a pleasure to hear, as her story rolled off her lips filling the air around us with the fear and terror of the morning of September 11.

When the first plane hit, she was on the phone talking to her sister. She heard a sound like a roaring subway train and then the building shuddered like a violent earthquake had struck. She didn't know what happened, so in order to get information she turned on the television and saw the second plane slam into the Tower. Her immediate concern was her children. Stuyvesant High School was closest and she arrived there quickly only to discover the students being evacuated. Her eldest daughter was in good hands, but she knew she had to get to her younger child, who she didn't think would be able to cope with what was happening. As she ran toward her daughter's school, the first Tower collapsed. It instantly became darker than night; she couldn't see where she was going. She said everybody was screaming and running. The woman told me after some of the darkness cleared she got to the school and found it in total chaos, with the children running all over the building wailing and emitting primeval screams. Her daughter was standing by the front door shaking and crying. She was so hysterical that she didn't even recognize her mother. The woman grabbed the girl and ran, until they were out of the neighborhood. The woman feared they were going to die. The child began to gag, so the mother stopped to assist her, when she realized they were covered with cement dust and some substance was sticking to them that gave them the appearance of a pair of ghosts. The child was choking from what had gotten lodged in her throat and nose. The woman leaned over and cleared the girl's mouth with her fingers, and then wrapped her sweater around the child, picked her up and kept running. Just north of White Street two police officers stepped into her path and stopped her. At that point, the mother and daughter were both hysterical and didn't want to stop running. The police had them transported to a hospital where they were treated for cuts and bruises, cleaned up, and released. They went to stay with a cousin on King Street north of Canal Street, but it was three anxious days before the family was reunited.

They had left their dog in the apartment because he was an old German shepherd, who couldn't run fast enough to escape and was too heavy to carry. After being reunited, the mother and her two daughters made plans to return to the apartment to claim their dog. Evacuation was the order of the day. The once beautiful neighborhood had become a crime scene with thousands of dead bodies and parts scattered throughout. The family was afraid the dog was hurt, or would starve to death, so they ignored the order and entered the forbidden Red Zone. Like many New Yorkers, they considered the dog part of the family. They infiltrated the barricades, got to the apartment building and together they took their dog and left. Her story made me wonder how secure the Red Zone was, or was it that the soldiers looked the other way at two kids and a mom trying to rescue a dog. The apartment windows had been open and all the debris had coated everything, painting a picture of total destruction. Their dog was frightened and was no longer black and tan, but a gruesome gray. He was hungry but excited to see his family and they were proud that they rescued him.

I gave her all I could to make things a little easier for her, but could only offer her my sympathy for the loss of her writings. She was grateful for the aid, but said she would live in fear for the rest of her life. She chose to seek private therapy for her traumatized daughters, so

I suggested to her our mental health services and she stated she would call us because she did want to take advantage of the offer.

After the woman left, I interviewed a young Greek limo driver, who took too much and wanted too much. The ripple effect had hit the community. He had a family of six and I did what I could for him.

The limo driver had hardly gotten up from the chair when another client sat in front of me. The first thing the young woman said to me was, "I know you will understand because you've been there." I didn't understand. I still don't understand. The supervisor was steering the Ground Zero clients to me. The woman had returned to tell us she left the hotel we had put her up in earlier and didn't want us to be charged. I phoned the hotel about their billing and was told that it was all automatic, so that we never were overcharged. I thanked them for allowing us to put people up in their establishment. They were courteous and said it was their pleasure to help the Red Cross. When I returned to the table, we just sat and talked. I also thanked her for her concern. I told her we could pay her rent if she got receipts for me, and she stated that she would return, but didn't feel she had any other emergency needs.

She was my last client for the day, and I was free to leave, so I walked through Tribeca past the Doggie Daycare and some delicious smelling restaurants to the subway. When I got back to Times Square, I walked to Staples to exchange my portfolio and then over to St. Patrick's for Mass. It was cold and the streets were crowded, but walking was a great stress reliever. After Mass, I stopped and watched the ice skaters at Rockefeller Center, and then I walked back to the hotel for dinner and a hot shower. I phoned home with the calling card that the Red Cross had given me. They were encouraging everyone to call home often because they felt it alleviated stress. Lou worked for Red Cross too and he knew how important the jobs were, so he was comfortable with my extension. "Do what you have to do," he told me in a supportive tone. He said things were going well at home and not to worry about anything. After I hung up, I wrote in my journal and went to bed. I was exhausted.

16 October 2001 – Tuesday
Manhattan, New York

Today my Chapter friends went home to Santa Rosa, California. I felt strange staying behind, but the day was busy and I soon forgot about it. Early in the morning a French woman with a Spanish name returned to see me. She had brought in the receipts I had requested, so we could make her mortgage payment. She was a young, chic professional architect, who was paying $5,000 a month for her apartment and never dreamed she would be asking anyone for assistance. She gave me an envelope full of pictures that she took from her apartment at Ground Zero. I offered to pay her for them, but she wouldn't hear of it. She couldn't live in her apartment yet because it wasn't habitable. Around the clock bright lights shone on the scene as the workers continued their hunt for bodies. Hazardous waste material coated the interior of the apartment, and then there was the issue of the smell. All her windows faced the scene and there would be no escape from the light, noise, or view, if she had to return. She was concerned because she couldn't break her lease, but didn't feel she could ever live there again.

The woman had been home working at the time of the attack and had taken shelter in the bathtub. She thought she was going to die. She complained to me that she had some sort of respiratory problem and was having difficulty breathing. She further complained of a constant cough. I wrote the proper form, and told her to stop by our nursing office before she left, and also to stop at mental health. She thanked me for being so kind.

I had four clients after that and I had to refuse them benefits. It wasn't our policy to turn people away, so I gave them referrals to other agencies where they might receive some sort of assistance. They came in one after another and didn't live or work in the Zone areas. It took a toll on me to turn people away.

As the day went on, I had an interesting case that required me to take a chance and leave myself open to getting into trouble with my superiors. A heavy-set single mom with dirty red hair, who lived close to the Twin Towers, came in for assistance. She was a quiet, nervous person who had a family of six young children one of which was sitting on her hip sucking his thumb and sleeping safe in his mother's arms. A day after the disaster she took her brood and snuck back into her apartment. I had just found out that to receive benefits the tenants had to be out at least five days. The family was living on a government subsidy and had nothing and nowhere else to go. They were all sick with respiratory problems from staying in the contaminated unit. The family was in serious trouble and was in desperate need of emergency assistance. They were going to fall through the cracks, if we didn't help them.

The woman was petrified that she would lose her children and was beside herself not knowing what to do. I chose to ignore the five-day rule and treated her no differently than the rest of the neighborhood. She kept thanking me and reached over with a great deal of affection and squeezed my hand. In the confusion, I accidentally made an enormous error in her favor on the grocery allotment, and hoped the paper trail wouldn't catch up with me. She came in with her neighbor, who had three children and a newborn infant, and they also had moved right back in for the same reasons. These people were poor and had no family, or place to go other than their apartments. They didn't know that the Red Cross would have given them hotel rooms, until they could recover. They were desperate and couldn't sleep on the streets, or in the park. The younger woman's baby was ill and another worker wouldn't even talk to her because she had not been out for five days. I would have liked to take that worker to Ground Zero and make her stay there for a day, just to smell the place and feel her aching lungs. I wasn't going to let those families end up homeless. They were so poor and feeling so hopeless besides being frightened that they would lose their children to the authorities for staying in their apartments. I put them up in hotels and referred them to our nursing staff. It was out of character for me to break the rules, but the humanitarian aspect of my personality reared its head and I had absolutely no choice but to help them.

The next client was an older black lady in a faded blue housedress with a barely visible design covered by a long thick red sweater that clung to the side of her large breasts. She was married to a self-employed truck driver, who delivered to the Trade Center, and the attack destroyed his business. She had photo identification passes to get in the Trade Center, but no proof of his employment. The woman was in shock and could hardly put her sentences together in a manner that made sense. The supervisor said she had to have a letter on company letterhead showing that her husband worked for those businesses before I could offer her our assistance. Now tell me, how does one do that when the companies are gone along with all the employees? I gave a disbursing order for groceries and told her to try to contact the main offices, so she could get the rest of her assistance. I also gave her a Red Cross bag full of cleaning supplies, candies, gloves, a teddy bear, and toiletries. She began to trust me and related her story.

That morning she went with her husband to the Trade Center in his truck. The woman wanted to pick up a book at Borders Books, stop and have coffee and maybe sit in the park to read for the rest of the morning. He dropped her off and decided to sit in the vehicle, finish his coffee and have a cigarette before his first delivery. She arrived at the Winter Garden several blocks away when she realized her good walking shoes were in the truck. It was still early, so she decided to walk back to the truck and exchange her shoes in order to have a more comfortable day. She knew her husband usually drank his coffee and planned out his day, so the truck would surely still be there. Suddenly, our world, as we know it, ended when the first jet slammed into the World Trade Center.

The woman was a diabetic, considerably overweight, and had bad feet, but she ran thinking she would escape if only she could get to the truck. She tripped and fell, and in the commotion, no one came to her aid. Her husband ran toward the scene, but couldn't find her because in a panic she had run the wrong direction. In total shock, she sat on a bench never dreaming the buildings were going to collapse. Again, she ran and then she fell to the ground. The woman went on to describe the sounds of screaming and the buildings falling. She said it sounded like a jet plane was coming directly at her. Jet fuel splashed down on two people near her, engulfing them both in flames. She said in a shaky voice that she could still hear them screaming. "A fireman appeared like an angel. He was kind to me, but we were both so scared. He saved me and I didn't even know who he was." He swiftly led her, partially carrying her for blocks to a waiting ambulance, which rushed from the scene to a hospital.

She sat in front of me and cried, as she attempted to deal with her emotions and guilt. "Why did those poor souls burn, and I didn't?" she said. I sympathized with her and told her we had people she could talk to who had wonderful advice on how to handle what she was going through. I always felt strange telling our clients that when we couldn't even imagine the pain they were enduring. The woman went to see the mental health staff and before she left she came back to my table, gave me a hug and thanked me for caring. I told her I would see her soon and not to forget to return for her other benefits.

I took a brief lunch break and walked around the neighborhood to clear my head. I seldom saw a child on the streets or in the stores. It was a community where the babies and children were prisoners in their own apartments. They lived behind tightly sealed windows to protect them from the insidious air. A few old men walked their dogs, stooping down to scoop up poop with tiny plastic bags. Barricades ringed the neighborhood making it difficult to get around. The streets weren't crowded and life had a long way to go before things would ever be back to normal. The "pile" was still burning and the air was so bad that it took on a life of its own. I only went a few blocks and then returned to the stuffy and crowded basement office. The air was not only rotten outside, but inside as well, so I just resigned myself to the situation, and went back to work.

I had two clients that were both limo drivers. One I assisted because his work was at the Trade Center and he had his trip tickets. The other I had to turn away because he didn't live or work anywhere near the area. I tried to give him referrals, but he didn't want them. He was so angry, and he kept staring at me, shaking a stack of unpaid bills in my face. He scared me, but I remained calm. A mental health worker saw I was having a problem and came to my rescue. We both tried to calm him down, but he left seething with rage. Many of the clients were moving from disbelief to an anger phase, and it was making the job more difficult, even dangerous.

The office had soft lights on the steep stairs that went to the first floor exit. Pictures encouraging laborers to stand up and fight for their rights lined the white brick walls. The place was gloomy. On the first floor side door where new clients entered, the security guard was nestled behind the marble counter sound asleep for which I couldn't blame him because his job was so boring. In the reception area, which was actually only a landing on the stairs, people were pushing their way in the door to register. They all wanted to make it downstairs to see a Family Service worker. Outside of the old-fashioned glass doors were long lines of potential clients. The front door around the corner was in better shape because only returning clients entered there and they were smaller in number. I thought it was possible that it could turn into a mob scene with tempers growing short and lines growing longer. It seemed like all Chinatown knew we were giving aid and everyone was showing up all at once from both sides of Canal Street. Chinatown radio had announced our presence and was encouraging the residents to see us for assistance. They came in droves.

I found the people from Chinatown, especially the women, to be sweet and bright. They liked me and I managed to stay on a personal level with them, even though we had to deal through interpreters. John, my supervisor, was superior because he advocated for the clients, and also had a good understanding of the volunteers. The two women supervisors were aloof and appeared to think they were better than any one else. Some of our workers were not in good physical shape, but they tried so hard and kept plodding along.

Two of our older volunteers fell. One broke her wrist and another broke a leg. I always felt that you had to work on your physical well being before you went out on jobs. The jobs were demanding and you had to keep in good shape, but some of our workers were quite elderly and it was difficult for them.

Starting tomorrow, our hours were going to change again, and I would be getting off later, but I had worked longer hours in the

Red Zone and didn't care. The change made it harder for the older workers.

After work I took the Metro to Times Square, and walked over to St. Patrick's for 5:30 p.m. Mass. I prayed for the missing, and that I would have the strength and wisdom to treat each client justly and with compassion. When the service began, the ushers roped off the Mass section and I got a reprieve from talking tourists and the annoying flashes from their cameras. I was amazed at how insensitive some people were taking pictures while a service was in progress. I wasn't sure when or if I would return to hear Mass with my new working hours. I reflected on the fact that I had to start making plans to leave New York soon.

After Mass, I ate dinner at Joe G's and basked in the quiet and privacy. I was cash broke and VISA made it possible for me to have a good meal. The pasta and pizza were delicious along with a couple of cold beers. I had time to write. The waiter packed me my usual bag of bread and cookies handing it to me with a tender smile. When I left New York, I gave him my Metro card as a small token of thanks for all his kindness toward me.

I was so tired, but glad I stayed on the job. They needed me and I really didn't feel done with what I came to do. I had grown to think that there was always one more family I could help.

17 October 2001 – Wednesday
Lower Manhattan

The place was an absolute madhouse today. When I got to work it was still dark and there were long, long lines down the block. They were all people from Chinatown, and it was a mob scene. We had to shove through the crowd to get into the front door. They pulled at our clothing, wanting us to notice them and let them in the building. They had been there since 1:00 a.m. It was frightening, but we pushed our way to the door and entered, escaping the crowd.

Once in the building we realized the toilets had backed up, and the entire basement stank like a septic tank that was long over-due for pumping. Without windows or ventilation it produced a difficult working space. The situation was creating tremendous stress. Clients and workers were growing short-tempered and irritable. The Red Cross officer in charge telephoned the police and they responded by putting up yellow tapes and saw horses to gain order among the waiting people before we had a riot on our hands. Lined up within the yellow tapes, the potential clients waited. The line extended for blocks, and I wondered if there was ever going to be an end to my job.

My new hours went into effect. I was due for a day off and my client, who had given me the photographs she had taken from her apartment, invited me to take a ride on the Staten Island Ferry. She said it was free, which was great because I was broke. I wasn't sure if I wanted to spend my day off doing that but told her I would think about it.

At my lunch break, I looked for a place to get my haircut. A client told me about a shop near the service center. I walked there only to find the prices starting at $95. Right $95! An old brick building housed a fancy beauty shop crowded with six hairdressers, who looked like they walked out of punk rock England, leather clothing complete with chains. They had body piercings, tattoos, and purple hair. I visualized my hair in pink spikes, and decided I would look elsewhere. I was so shaggy that I couldn't stand it anymore, but I knew I would perhaps find a more reasonable place in Times Square near the hotel.

After lunch, I returned to work with my Asian clients. I had never worked with Chinese people before, and after the job was over I had a trip to China planned. Mostly, we were dealing with very poor, uneducated people, but in China I was to see how they all lived and hoped it would broaden my mind and help me understand their culture and family structure.

Assigned to me for the afternoon was a young Chinese Mormon male interpreter. I was pleased because at past national jobs, I had found the Mormons to be hardworking people with good attitudes. I was always happy to see them. A woman came in, who worked in the garment industry in Chinatown. She was elderly and smelled of Clorox, and breath mints. I noticed as I shook her sweating hand that she was shaking. I had the interpreter explain that we were there to assist her and she need not be nervous. I made sure she understood that we were not a government agency. Many undocumented workers thought Red Cross was government and were afraid. [Red Cross has no concerns regarding a person's legal status.] I knew she was in desperate straits, but I admired her courage for coming in to see us. I wrote out disbursing orders and took care of her immediate emergency needs. She thanked me and apologized for taking my time. I hated the language barrier because I couldn't get close to the clients. I touched the woman's bony, age spotted hands and looked into her eyes when I spoke to the interpreter, so she would understand that I cared deeply about her well being. The woman was so humble and quiet as I asked why she hadn't applied for unemployment insurance. She stated that her employer told her she couldn't. He would not allow it, which was ridiculous. Many of the women in that industry were petrified of their employers. They worked for slave wages, and I was sure the working conditions weren't up to standard. It was amazing that some of them didn't step forward and fight for their civil rights. Hopefully someone has and I am just not aware of it. I would check their pay stubs and be dumbfounded as to how they survived in New York City with a family, on so little money.

Another Chinese man was my next client. He was returning a disbursing order made out to his landlord and wanted us to change the landlord's name to a different name, which we wouldn't do. It was a misunderstanding on my part, because in his dialect the name was spelled differently and appeared to be a different name altogether. My interpreter explained that we were working with several dialects, the two main ones being Mandarin and Cantonese. Also, there were other dialects that even he didn't understand. The man's request was legitimate, so I redid the paperwork and he left smiling, thanking me.

The interpreter was a college professor who taught Chinese culture and history, so I had the opportunity to question him on the Chinese people and their customs. He said it was okay to look a Chinese person in the eye when speaking and that the Chinese read your facial expressions. He said they liked me because I was kind and interested in them. He was a great help to me.

When my supervisor saw my interpreter move on to assist another caseworker, he brought a short, older woman named Sara to my table. Sara stood in front of me, in the crowded madhouse of a basement, with her Red Cross vest, her shoulder length, white curly hair, and her tiny stature, with a spaced-out glare in her sky blue eyes. Sara had become part of my job, and she was to sit with me as I followed orders to train her. She was a mental health worker who had gone out on this job as a Family Service worker and had no idea what she was doing. Thanks loads, John! She never stopped talking and didn't pay attention to the clients, or my instructions. Sara had just arrived and was staying at my hotel. She had come on the job yesterday, but spent the day at headquarters getting her assignment. Sara, with an adrenaline level of ten, never stopped chattering and asking inappropriate questions, which slowed me down. I tried my utmost to be nice, but she attached herself to me like a barnacle, even following me to the bathroom. When I finished with my last client, a Chinese merchant, I told her I would show her to the subway. In a way I felt sorry for her. She had planned to go out to dinner with me, so I could continue her instructions. Anyway, that was a problem that didn't come about because the supervisor told her she would have to work till 10:00 p.m. She had a fit, saying she didn't work long hours and that she had a headache. The old gal told the supervisor that I had to teach her. She liked me and wanted me to stay with her. I explained that I was a technician and that she had to follow the instructions her supervisor gave to her. I was willing to let her watch me work, but God forbid, follow me into my private space – I think not.

I was no longer able to attend Mass with the change of hours, but I got there whenever possible. After work I took the subway back to the hotel. Many blacks and Puerto Ricans took the same train. I was accustomed to hearing the Spanish language, but when I heard the Puerto Ricans, I didn't understand their Spanish. They had a dialect that was so strange to me. I stood sandwiched up against my fellow passengers, as the train headed to 59th Street. I was holding onto a pole for balance when I noticed also grasping the same pole was a gnarled black hand, a small yellow hand, a brown hand, and my white hand. I realized the diversity of the cosmopolitan atmosphere where I grew up in San Francisco was missing in my life, with all its richness, now that I lived in the North Bay. The vast majority of the passengers had some sort of headset on, listening to music to make the ride more pleasant. I, like the other passengers, drifted off into my own world where I began to make plans about what I would do on my day off that would be within the constraints of my aching budget.

18 October 2001 – Thursday
Manhattan, New York

Today was my day off, but I forgot until I woke up and remembered it was Thursday. I had to get up at 5:30 a.m., go to the lobby, and tell John and Herbert I wouldn't be going in and not to wait for me. They left for work and I went back upstairs and went to sleep with my clothes on for a couple of hours. I decided against the trip to Staten Island because I wanted to be alone. When I woke up, I walked to the Guggenheim Museum on 88th Street and 5th Avenue, which was a long walk with a bitter cold wind. On arriving there, I discovered the museum was closed and, rather than return to the Metropolitan Museum across the street, I chose to walk back to the hotel. I enjoyed the walk, admiring the magnificent buildings, statues, fountains, and even watching the vendors and just the general life in the city. At the hotel, I picked up another sweater and walked to Broadway to try and find some more of the large photos of Ground Zero, but they were out of stock.

I saw a Gray Line double-decker bus on a loop tour. I hopped on, flashed my Red Cross identification and settled down for a free two-hour tour. The top deck looked inviting, but I sat inside because it was warmer. The present environment in Manhattan, with its many blocked off streets, wasn't conducive to tour busses. Traffic was snarled and very slow, as our bus crawled through Greenwich Village and

Soho. The baritone voice on the microphone blasting throughout the bus told me that only artists were allowed to rent apartments in Soho and Greenwich Village, and I wondered who determined that. As we approached the United Nations it had the security of an armed camp, just like the Zone. We passed 34th Street and the biggest Macy's I'd ever seen, and the skyscrapers were endless. No one spoke to me and I was content with that. Chinatown was also off limits to the bus. More Asians than Italians occupied the district called Little Italy. The Italian immigration to New York had been fifty years earlier and the present immigrants were mostly Asians. The Italian population had blended into New York, and many had moved to San Francisco and elsewhere.

When the bus pulled back to the hotel, I jumped off and walked to a nearby deli where I bought food to bring back to my room. I spent the rest of the day watching the rented movie, *Pearl Harbor*. It was long, but a good story. When the movie ended, I took a Celebrex because I irritated an old injury in my foot with the long walk. I got my black coat and headed for St. Patrick's on 49th Street and 5th Avenue. Before Mass, I walked through some of the shops in Rockefeller Center, and noticed how everything was so expensive. But there was little escape from the tension, as fire trucks roared by with Hazmat emergency vehicles following close behind, and detectives in unmarked cars with small flashing red lights on their vehicle roofs.

After Mass, I returned to the hotel and stopped at the business center to email my close friend Father Serge Propst. That was a gas. I went into the business office and I was so tired I forgot my password and couldn't retrieve my mail. I was having difficulty concentrating. I was getting very tired both emotionally and physically. My emotions didn't bother me if I was working and busy, but when I was alone it was hard to deal with all that had happened. I had seen and heard too much. The television constantly replayed the attacks and there was really no place to escape the tension.

I didn't need dinner, but always pampered myself on my Red Cross days off. I went to the Italian restaurant for a big meal and sat in back to escape the smoking clientele. There was a group of old Sicilian men sitting at a large round table, who rattled away in a mixture of Sicilian and English. As they ate their pasta and drank their red wine, they began to shout at each other, until one of them pulled out a deck of cards. The waiter cleared off their plates and the card game began. It was like a set from the *Godfather* movie, but in real life. I enjoyed my dinner as I wrote my thoughts on scratch paper. When I finished, I returned to the hotel, took a hot shower, and went right to sleep.

19 Friday 2001 – Friday
Lower Manhattan, New York

I went to work with Herbert and John at 5:45 a.m. and when we arrived long lines of potential clients were already waiting in the dark outside the front door. At the staff meeting, there was a great concern expressed about the Anthrax scare. A lockdown of our facility was the word from above. I visualized myself taking up residence in the basement with dozens of people and no toilets. The toilets still weren't working and the office smelled worse than the smoke outside. There was no fresh air for us anywhere. The toilet on the third floor was available, but not to the clients. I pondered what they were doing about that especially the ones who had been outside waiting all night. Three plumbers came in around ten o'clock and worked in the downstairs basement bathroom, pumping mysterious substances out of the six toilets next to our office and hauling it out in large black plastic garbage bags. It stirred up the odor to a point that clients were sitting with cloths over their faces. By the end of my shift, they still had not repaired the problem. They said there were just too many people in the building, and the old plumbing system couldn't handle it. So, now I smelled like shit.

We were given information for emergency situations telling us that in these times of high alert and need for awareness, the following actions were recommended to all staff assigned the DR 787 (Disaster Response 787). They told us to remain where we were and take instructions from the authorities, for local volunteers to stay home unless already at work; they gave us phone numbers to call to report our location, to make sure we had a work buddy and contact each other once a day, call home often; and they gave us a phone number for medical questions. So, now we had to worry about a chemical or biological attack which was in the back of our minds anyway along with everything else.

The day was very crowded with almost all of our clients being from Chinatown. Chinese radio again had announced to the public that the Red Cross was giving benefits and giving our location and hours. We couldn't have made it without the generosity of our local volunteer translators.

As the day wore on, the air outside was almost unbearable. The "pile" was only about six blocks from the service center. The cranes opened another pocket and found seven bodies. It hung over us all like a cloak of depression digging into our already sore throats and aching lungs. I opted to smell the smoke instead of the toilet and walked down to the barricades. I needed to leave at lunchtime because the basement had no windows and I didn't even know what the weather was like. I hadn't seen daylight yet that day. It was hard to believe the "pile" was burning, but it was and someone told me it was the jet fuel and it would probably burn for months.

When I returned to work, a man from Battery Park came in to see me. He needed assistance with his rent and security deposit. He had lived in the Red Zone and couldn't return to his home. He found another apartment but because of the location of his first apartment, we paid. The rent was $4500 with a $4000 security deposit. We stipulated the security deposit be returned to the American Red Cross whenever he chose to move.

I had to make sure, if we paid the $8500 that he would be able to pay his rent in the future. He was an architect and was well able to maintain the apartment. People made remarks to me about the "rich yuppies" in Manhattan and asked why we assisted them with a greater amount of rent. The young professionals had bigger salaries, bigger debts. Everything was relative. By being there, I observed that if a family paid $800 a month rent and earned a smaller salary, it was proportional. We met the emergency needs of the people at the level which they were living. The suffering was a different issue. Economic level played no role in the misery of the people in Manhattan. They all suffered.

The architect told me his story of how his two young children had witnessed the people jumping out of the buildings. He was beside himself with worry, and didn't know how to cope with the stress his children were undergoing. He asked me for mental health assistance, which was not a problem being that we had mental health staff right at the service center. I couldn't get his file because he had gone to another service center originally, and they were in the process of moving. I told him I would track down his records and to please return in a couple of days, but first to stop at mental health on his way out. He thanked me and told me it would be no problem to return.

As he left I had a moment to catch my breath and began thinking about all the neighborhood children I had seen. Witnessing the attack had traumatized them. They were affectionately called "Window Walkers", the young children who walked back and forth in front of their apartment windows on a daily basis. The poor little window walkers had seen all the violence, felt all the shock, and were processing it like children did. Their childhood crumbled along with the Towers, their young innocence stolen from them that sunny morning. They were petrified, insecure, and falling apart. Our mental health teams worked with many of the children, but you couldn't help thinking about what was ahead in their future. For me the hardest part of the job was seeing the children suffer.

I interviewed a couple of more clients before my day finally ended. I left work alone and headed for the crowded subway. I boarded the train, packed in the car with a population escaping various offices, my body stacked up against strangers. It was stuffy with the odors of perfumes, shaving lotions, and perspiration all blended together. When I got off the train I had to wait to exit the underground because the stairways were so narrow that they couldn't contain all the people. I was convinced that the subway was the most dangerous place in New York, being an ideal location for another terrorist attack.

One of the mental health workers was going home Saturday. She and her coworker decided to have dinner with me at the Italian restaurant.

I told them I would meet them at Joe G's. It was only the second time I had eaten with anyone after work. The waiter and the bartender looked at me with a curious smile when I walked into the restaurant with two companions. I was so reclusive in their establishment that they probably thought I had few friends. The workers interrogated me regarding my work in the Red Zone. I got a glimpse into the future regarding the many years I would have to go over and over the pain we endured there. Other than that we had a pleasant dinner, said our good-byes, and I went back to the hotel and to bed. I was nervous and turned the television on softly to keep me company. It played and replayed the terrorist strike and interviews with victims, families, fire, and police and kept repeating the same thing over and over. I slept off and on all night.

20 October 2001 – Saturday
Manhattan, New York

I arrived at the service center at 6:30 a.m. to a line of about 250 people. As I gazed at the long line, it occurred to me to wonder whether we were actually doing any good. We had a staff meeting after which I went to nursing to get something for my throat. The smoke was intense, just pouring out of the Trade Center site blocking out the dawn sky, and making me feel like I was smoking a couple of packs of cigarettes a day. The nurse told me to get a base line x-ray when I returned home because of the daily exposure to the pollutants and asbestos in the air, but she had no masks to offer, just cough drops. She said she believed the air was safe and I felt like a child with inconsistent parents. No one ever got the story straight about the air, and every day my cough grew worse. I never developed a fever and didn't feel ill, so it didn't interfere with my job, but I wondered what the long-term affects were going to be and if anyone would ever care.

I took one case at a time and hoped that some of the people were genuine victims of 9/11. We couldn't judge anyone and had to treat everyone equally, something which I kept reminding myself of as I worked. I met with one garment worker after another, all women, all sweet, docile, and all poor. We paid their rent, groceries, and gave them Family Allowance Grants. Those poor souls were living from hand to mouth. It was also interesting to me that most of their husbands were twenty to forty years their senior. Many lived in fear of the terrorists, their bosses, and in some cases their spouses. It was difficult to see women so suppressed living right in America. It was interesting to me that most of the garment workers had American passports and were very proud of them. I never asked to see anyone's passport, but they often showed them to me anyway.

At noon, when I decided to take a break, a difficult situation arose for me. After spending the morning interviewing people, I decided to take a walk down toward the lower part of Harrison Street, which was only two blocks away. There was an enormous bulldozer working behind the barricade in the Zone. I stood in the sun and watched for awhile and decided to ask the police officer guarding the blockade what they were going to do with all the concrete the bulldozer was moving to the waiting trucks. I walked over to the officer and he stated in a thick Brooklyn accent that the debris was picked up, put on a barge, and taken to Fresh Kill Landfill at Staten Island where all of it was gone through bit by bit looking for body parts, watches, rings, or other personal effects. We were standing in a cloud of dust as the bulldozer dropped big scoops of debris onto waiting trucks. A Red Cross Mass Care worker, a short, balding blond older man with a large belly protruding from his work vest and a video camera propped on his shoulder approached us. He flashed his Red Cross badge with his thumb neatly tucked over the yellow strip that stated he didn't have access to Ground Zero. I couldn't believe my eyes. The rookie was impressed with the man's badge and told him if he had to take pictures to please hurry. Then the crummy-looking Mass Care worker aimed his video camera at the bulldozer. His plump wife, in her Red Cross work vest, who was right behind him, took out a disposable point and shoot camera and they began taking pictures. They were like two jackals going in for the kill, and nothing was going to stop them. Red Cross in the Red Zone allowed no photography, and they understood that. I knew what the bulldozer was moving, and I put our workers in a not much better category than paparazzi. Those Red Cross workers showed no respect for the dead. They were only interested in bringing home a souvenir video and some snapshots. Red Cross was the only disaster relief in the country sanctioned by Congress. With people like that couple and their unacceptable behavior, the Red Cross could lose their privileges of going to the ground zeros of the world, and thousands of individuals would not receive the much needed assistance that we had to offer. I warned them but they wouldn't stop, as they laughed at both the police officer and me. He tried to get them to hurry, but they refused and continued on taking pictures from every angle imaginable. The couple should have been relieved of their duty and sent home. As a group we had an obligation to protect Red Cross, so the organization would continue to function in the same capacity. I was disgusted.

I couldn't stand watching them anymore so I returned to the office to the endless line of victims. My first case after lunch was from further in the Red Zone. The client was a tall slender woman with an Italian accent, who was out of the country on business when the incident occurred. She took the first plane available back to New York. There was no way she could reach her apartment that first week because of the barricades, so she waited and worried. She stayed in upper Manhattan on 42nd Street at the Grand Hyatt, until the word was out that the residences could return for short periods of time to claim their belongings. She immediately went to the barricades. The young woman had to wait in a line while people showed the soldiers at the fence their drivers' licenses, department store bills, Con Edison bills, anything that would prove they lived in the area. Having a current New York driver's license showing her address, she was allowed to pass. There was no transportation, so she walked to her apartment, only to find it and everything in it destroyed. The blown in windows caused fine dirt and broken glass to scatter throughout her residence. The woman told me that despite all of that she felt fortunate because she had a trunk full of clothing coming in from overseas, and she hadn't lost her laptop, or her business files. Considering what had happened, the woman had an incredible calmness about her. What bothered her most was that she would probably never have her neighborhood back. Who was going to return? They were all terrified and wanted to leave the area as soon as possible. She asked, "How long will it burn? When will the air be safe?" I had no answers.

Living alone and having to find a new apartment in Manhattan was difficult. We sat and talked while I wrote the narrative on the case file. She took a brown teddy bear off of the table and hugged it while she spoke. The woman said the Red Cross was wonderful and when she got back on her feet she was going to return every cent. I explained where the money had come from and that it was free, but she insisted because to her it was a loan. She was determined to recover as quickly as possible and only asked for immediate emergency assistance, which I was glad to arrange for her. As she left still clutching the bear, she said, "God Bless all of you for being here."

I went to Records and Reports and turned in the case file and when I returned, the little lady, Sara, was waiting at my table. I had gotten used to her and accepted her for what she was. I felt sorry for her because she had no friends and was lonely. Sara had experience in mental health, and it was amusing to watch a client try to torture her, because it never worked. People couldn't push her buttons, but her paperwork was always exasperating. I tried to help her when I could and worked well with her. I explained the papers to her many times, but to no avail. She would get in the line for the supervisor's approval and remain there for a long time trying to correct her mistakes.

Sara was off talking to a supervisor when a young man sat down at my table. He had been in the Trade Center when the second plane hit, and he was anxious to tell me his story about how he ran down flights and flights of stairs as firemen ran up. When he escaped, he thought about the firemen he had seen going in the building, and decided to return to be of assistance to those who had not yet escaped. Then the building began to collapse; he ran for his life. He made it out and kept running. As he continued he said he saw paper, and all sorts of debris flying throughout the air. People were screaming and stampeding down the street heading toward Broadway Street. Then the infamous cloud of dust darkened everything. He dropped to the ground, covered his head, and rolled into a ball. When the cloud passed, color was gone from the world; everything was gray. He found himself covered with dust and bloody cuts on his body, a banshee. At first, he thought he was dead until the dirt and debris in his mouth began to choke him. He spit and gagged and then tried to stand up. He put his hand on the person next to him for balance. The only problem was the person was only the torso of a person, and as he told me he became silent and stared straight ahead with vacant brown eyes swimming with tears. He was reflecting on something I could only imagine. I tried to signal mental health because I didn't feel I could leave him, and I wasn't sure what he was going to do. He was clutching both his hands as if he were hanging onto something I couldn't see. He began to talk again and told me his entire office staff was missing. What was he going to do? I spent an hour with him, and mental health joined us. I couldn't leave because they preferred we stay, so the client wouldn't feel uncomfortable, or deserted. There was so much human suffering and it was so difficult to be strong when inside I wept.

When I left for the day there were so many stories swimming around in my head that I felt like I was drowning in them. I walked through the neighborhood past the Doggie Day Care where people picked up their dogs at the end of the day, and past the restaurants packing their cars for dinner deliveries to the various apartments. Finally, I boarded the subway. The train stopped in the tunnel for ten minutes right before our station. It was common for the trains to stop, but no one explained what was going on and the people were getting nervous, trapped. It didn't take much to make the people jumpy because they were all waiting for something else to happen. Then the train started up and we arrived safely at the 59th Street Station.

When I returned to the hotel and was preparing for my shower, I noticed that I had developed the strangest rash around my waist from the constant exposure to dirt. When I washed my underclothes out at night, the water in the sink was black. I longed for a clean environment. I was so tired that I forgot to eat and went directly to bed.

21 October 2001 – Sunday
Manhattan, New York

We had an early staff meeting in the basement. After the meeting, I unloaded an ERV full of snacks for the clients and workers. The Mass Care worker appreciated my help and I was glad for a change of routine. The line had grown in length, and our working conditions continued to deteriorate with the toilet situation not improving. I took a couple of clients and slaved over mountains of trip tickets trying to calculate the before and after economic conditions of two limo drivers. It got to be about eleven o'clock and I told the supervisor that I was taking an early lunch and needed to go for a walk. He told me to take my time because I had been working so hard.

I left the building by the front door, so I wouldn't have to mill my way through the waiting crowd. I walked through the neighborhood near Chambers Street. Manhattan was like a series of little villages, distinct neighborhoods that had a unique character to each. There were small parks surrounded by skyscrapers. There were no single-family dwellings like in other cities. I had to purchase a NYPD cap for Al Phillips at my home Chapter who was a retired San Francisco police officer and a good friend. I stopped at a vendor's stand, which sold every kind of hat imaginable, framed pictures of the attack and its aftermath, scarves and knit hats with American flag designs singing out from their acrylic fabric where I purchased the NYPD cap.

The barricades were at every turn, slicing neighborhoods like wedges of pie, making it difficult for traffic and pedestrians to go about their daily business. Staring straight ahead the crowds gathered at the barricades, subdued and strangely silent, speaking only in the hushed tones used when in a church, or a library. No one even looked at me because they had grown accustomed to uniformed personnel in the neighborhood. I passed the photo store with the picture of the people jumping from the Tower. They had enlarged it and you could see people holding hands as they jumped to their deaths. The photograph had been enlarged many times its normal size in an attempt to identify the jumpers. I looked at the picture and wondered what alternative they had other than to jump. Small snapshots of everything you could imagine at the site were for sale for five dollars each. I stepped inside and purchased five of the photos. The merchant took them from large stacks that he kept in a glass case covered with greasy fingerprints from previous customers.

When I arrived back at work, I knew before I turned the corner to the side door that there would be hundreds of people, and there were. I worked my way through the crowd to the entrance. People were pulling at my clothing trying to tell me their stories, why they should see me first, and how long they had been waiting. They spoke English, but not well enough to interview. Their comprehension level was not good, so I needed the translator for the vast majority of my cases, which added to the stress. I actually had to instruct some of the interpreters to tell the clients exactly what I was saying and not to embellish it with information that was not necessary.

As I went down into the basement, I spotted an attractive white woman sitting in the waiting area continually wiping her red face with Kleenex. When I noticed she was in distress, I took her first. As she sat at my table, she blurted out that it was her first job and she was working as an administrative assistant on the 35th floor of one of the Towers when the first plane hit. There had been an announcement to stay in the office, but the employees were too frightened to obey and headed for the exits. She said there was an eerie calm among her coworkers as they tried to escape down flights of stairs. The building shuddered like a wounded animal moaning, whining, and the stairs began to give way. There was a collapse leaving only a small opening between the stairs and one of the halls, so she and a couple of her coworkers started pulling people through a circular space to free them. Things were falling around her, and she thought they had gotten everyone out. Most of them had jumped to a safer section and continued on down the stairs, but she heard a woman screaming for help so she and her friend tried to pull the woman through the opening. The woman was too large to fit as they kept trying to free her. Finally, they realized they couldn't save her, or they would die, so they left the woman behind. She told me that every night in her dreams she heard the woman's pleas not to leave her. The young woman's guilt encompassed her. I was amazed that she escaped considering the building was collapsing around her.

As my client neared the lobby, her ankle gave out and a police officer picked her up and carried her outside. Her hands were bleeding and she was covered with dirt when she reached the safety of the ambulance. She was not to be consoled as she sobbed. I had such a hard time not crying, but it was imperative that I be strong in order to be affective. Mental Health came over and asked me not to leave. I couldn't have left even if I wanted to because the woman had an iron grip on my hand. We spent a painful forty-five minutes with her. Would she ever recover from such a shock and such guilt? How would she manage? How could I make sense out of all that was happening?

Some of the workers including Sara asked if we could go to Mass at noon at St. Andrew's, a nearby church. The supervisor said he couldn't spare us for even an hour. He told us we were working till 8:30 p.m. I had gotten there at 6:30 a.m., so that made a 14-hour day, but I didn't say anything and went back to work. He never said anything if we asked to go to lunch and I found that strange. Sara, on the other hand, did what she pleased most of the time and this was no exception. Sara went anyway and brought me back a church bulletin from the previous Sunday Mass that had an insert from Father James Hayes of St. Andrew's neatly tucked inside. I had no idea that we would become friends, but fate is a strange thing and unbeknownst to Sara she had done me a huge favor giving me one of the best friends I was to ever have. (I was to meet this priest on my second return to this job in January and February.)

The word came down from management that we would cut off aid to everyone that didn't live in the Zone. Anger reared its ugly head all around us. I can't really blame the Red Cross for such a decision because everything was so new and the rules for everyone were changing every day.

A taxi driver came in and sat across from me shaking his bills in my face and telling me I had to pay them. I explained I couldn't because we had stopped offering assistance, unless the client lived in the Zone. "I have a family. You have to help me. We are desperate", the man begged.

I got an interpreter to make sure he understood what I was saying. He had horrendous anger in his eyes. "I don't need a damn interpreter. You can't do this to me, you bitch." The situation was getting volatile, so I left the man with the interpreter and got a mental health worker. The three of us tried to calm him down, but didn't succeed. He refused any referrals I tried to give him. He finally left, cursing us all the way out the door. His behavior brought back memories of the angry woman in Houston who had pulled a gun on the family services worker after the Tropical Storm Allison had hit that area. But I felt in my heart that the taxi driver had a legitimate complaint, whereas the woman in Texas did not.

My worst experience came in the form of an African-American man who turned up in the late afternoon. He was a middle-aged family man who had worked at Ground Zero in the Marriott Hotel for fifteen years. He had on a blue button-down dress shirt and clean khaki slacks with a knit cap on his head completely covering his hair and accenting his large, sad brown eyes. He didn't live in the Zone, so I had to refuse him Red Cross assistance. What good did it do to give a destitute man referrals, when he needed assistance immediately? He was so broke that he begged me for a token, so he could ride the subway. Humanitarianism was suppressed by rules that came down from people who weren't out in the field and didn't have to look into the eyes of that broken and desperate individual. He broke my heart, and I felt helpless. The Americorps girl working with me stormed off from our table frustrated, and not knowing what to do. The mental health worker, who spoke to him ended up in tears. He was one step away from the man who slept on the train, through no fault of his own. I will never as long as I live forget the look in that man's eyes, nor forgive myself for not breaking the rules and helping him. The tension among my coworkers was explosive. One of my young male cohorts ran out of the building and chased the man down. He gave him the money for the subway ride, but nothing more.

Management told us not to wear our Red Cross clothing in public because we were possible targets of an angry segment of the community. I didn't pay much attention to previous warnings because all I had brought with me was my Red Cross jacket, and in the Red Zone it was a requirement. I did have my heavy new black coat in the hotel. But, this warning I heeded because some of the people I turned away were on the verge of violence. I felt not obeying the order posed a threat to my safety. With street clothing on, I just blended into the crowd and hoped none of the angry clients remembered what I looked like.

My last client of the day was a fifty-year-old eastern European woman who lived with her adult son. I called her name and she slowly walked over and sat down in front of me. Her face was drawn and she told me she wasn't sleeping, and couldn't erase the fear from her mind that it was going to happen again. She requested assistance with her rent, food, and utilities. She told me that her son was working at the Trade Center and had escaped right after the first plane hit. He told her that people ran so fast they left their shoes behind. I knew that to be true because many clients had told me the same thing. She didn't know what happened until it was over, but stated that she thought it was a bomb, or a serious earthquake. The woman hid in the laundry room of her apartment house petrified with fear. When she heard what had happened she thought her son was dead because she was unable to contact him for hours. There was an immediate evacuation of the neighborhood. Also, the building and surrounding area was a crime scene and the authorities didn't want anyone in the vicinity, except for emergency personnel. Her son no longer had a place of employment and she told me he was trying to make sense out of why most of his coworkers were dead, and he was still alive. They no longer had a place to live, all their food was spoiled, and their apartment was destroyed, including their computers, furniture, and clothing. They had so many issues that I didn't know where to begin. I listened with compassion to her story, and tried to understand, but it was difficult. The clients thought we understood everything and I understood nothing. How was I supposed to understand why all of these people were suffering the way they were. I didn't know. Their finances would recover, but I wondered if they would mentally recover. Would they ever get over such a thing? How would they put their lives back together?

I left the office late after a long day, only to discover a bomb threat closed the subway, which put me on a Metro bus for the first time. It was crowded, but they took the same Metro pass as the subway, which was convenient. In fact, I enjoyed riding above ground because I got to see more of the city and got a better understanding of the bus system. I never heard what went on in the subway but assumed it was a false alarm – another one.

22 October 2001 – Monday
Manhattan, New York

I took the subway into work with John and Herbert, and there was no evidence that there had been any trouble. It was open and our predawn ride was uneventful. When we arrived at the service center, the long lines had already formed at the side of the building, and the guard remained behind the locked door cowering behind his desk. A big semi truck from Mass Care pulled up in front of the service center's side door with 500 five gallon buckets full of supplies for our clients. Each bucket contained cleaning supplies, teddy bears, personal hygiene articles, and snacks. We made a human chain and unloaded. I put the 500 buckets from the truck down onto the street, and the other workers hauled them downstairs to our basement. It felt wonderful to work, until I was soaked in perspiration. Physical work was great for relieve of stress, plus I needed the exercise. I loved working in the Family Services section of Red Cross, but also enjoyed Mass Care. Mass Care was hard physical labor, but it carried much less mental stress with it.

After we unloaded the truck, we had a late staff meeting. The job officer told us we had handled 3,330 cases in our service center to date and spent $3,211,000. The job had easily turned into a Category Five operation. The expenditures on the operation determined the category level. Of course, the expenditures on this job were beyond belief, and no one knew how high they were to go, or when they would level off.

The management also informed us of another change. We could now take care of anyone that worked or lived south of Canal Street. The

African-American man I turned away haunted me. He would appear in my dreams and was sure to stay with me for the rest of my life. As a human being, I failed him. I replayed over and over the different steps I could have taken to be of assistance to him, and each one required breaking the rules, and I didn't.

The basement office was so crowded that it was as hot as the subway. I worked all morning with an interpreter and one Chinese client after another. One Chinese woman who was a garment worker sat at my table with the translator. It was routine what we gave her. I tried to focus on each client and give him or her my full attention. She took my hands and said in very broken English, "Thank you. Thank you". Then she pushed an American passport over to me and said, "I – am – an – American". I think that was all the English she knew, but she was so sincere and her eyes danced with pride. She touched my heart.

Another garment worker came in, but there was something different about her. She was attractive, bright and didn't look as beaten down as all the others. My translator and I encouraged her to go to school to learn English. Her two teenaged daughters spoke English and could help her. There was no future in the garment industry because everything was closing. The interpreter told her the name of local schools where she could undertake such an endeavor. She looked up from the table and her brown eyes sparkled with excitement. She agreed that she would go to school. As we talked, I found out that in her country she had been a registered nurse and was a well-educated woman. She just needed some time and someone to show her compassion and understanding. I gave her the standard disbursing orders, for which she was grateful, but most of all we were able to lift the veil of darkness and despair in her life by giving her hope. She was one of my few clients that left the office happy and with the seed of a new idea in her mind, something she was anxious to nurture.

At lunch, I went for a walk up Duane Street and saw another firehouse in mourning with a flag at half-mast flying from their second-story window. There were pictures of the fallen heroes outside the station. Propped up in front of the pictures were roses, daisies and variegated bunches of flowers some in vases, some still in the plastic wrap tied with yellow or pink ribbons. People also had left cards and letters of condolences. Engine 7 had not lost a fireman in the incident but took in the remaining firefighters from Engine 10 who lost everyone on duty the morning of the attack. Engine 10 was directly across the street from the Towers. The doors of Engine 7 ladder 1 were open and eight large cardboard boxes full of shirts were lying on the floor by the fire engines. The firemen were selling them to raise money for the widows and orphans of their fallen brothers. The back of the shirts had a picture of the firemen raising the American flag at the pile with the words, "Strength and Honor". On the bottom of the picture was the date, September 11. On the front was a logo that said, "In memory of New York City's Bravest – Pride, Honor, Courage – for those who lost their lives in the line of duty". The shirts were expensive but I bought two and considered it a donation to a good cause.

After lunch, I returned to the office. It was crowded and the air was stale and thick, a soup of disgusting odors, a mixture of feces and perspiration. I processed five garment workers throughout the afternoon, but had little interaction with them because of the language barrier. I was sure it was just as frustrating for them as it was for me. They brought their fears to the table and there was nothing I could say to calm them. Often I would hold their hand, or hug them when they left. I did the best I could, but wanted to do more.

I decided to go out with Sara after work because she was so lonesome. So, we ate a delicious dinner at the Italian restaurant. Sara was so short that when she sat down on the wooden restaurant chair her feet didn't touch the floor. She talked incessantly about her family, her home and our job. She had a big appetite, wolfing down pasta, a pizza, and two beers. When we paid the bill and were ready to leave the waiter gave me a small white bag full of cookies, cheeses and some bread for work the next day. I think that restaurant sort of adopted me.

After dinner, we decided to take a long walk before returning to the hotel for the evening. We went down Broadway to Times Square, which was all lit up in American glory. There was a vibrancy and energy there that was exciting and all embracing. Sara hadn't been anywhere because she had no one to go with. She was not quite five feet tall, elderly, and vulnerable. She was bouncing around like a child; she was so excited about walking down to Broadway. We walked over to the Engine Company 54 Ladder 4 on 8th Avenue where she signed the condolence book that was on a podium in front of the firehouse door. It took her twenty minutes, to write her comments. I would have loved to read them.

As we continued our walk, she almost died of shock when she saw a person who was obviously a man dressed as a woman soliciting business on the corner. I herded her around like a watchful border collie so she wouldn't get herself into trouble. She bought bulky sweaters from a vendor for one dollar each. They were stacked higher than Sara could see and were all colors and sizes. She bought five and then had to carry them. I bought one to comply with the new order not to wear Red Cross clothing on the streets. It was fun to watch her because she had the innocence of a child and she enjoyed everything. I had grown much attached to her and her sarcastic sense of humor.

When we got back to the hotel, I said good night to Sara and took the elevator up to my room. I called home and made a doctor's appointment to check my lungs. The nurses on the job said the air was safe, but I didn't believe them. The EPA report would say one day the air was safe, and the next day it wasn't. At Ground Zero I had a lightweight surgical-type mask. At the end of the day it was dirty both inside and out, so it was basically useless. At the new job with the same air, masks were never mentioned and not available to us. I still had a few in my carry-on that I had picked up along the way. The only effective mask would have been a respirator and they weren't available either.

I was exhausted, took a hot shower, and went right to bed.

23 October 2001 – Tuesday
Lower Manhattan, New York

They took out more bodies today and the rank smoke was dense controlling the mood of the neighborhood. The center wasn't much better, as the anger and impatience grew among the clients. The rules kept changing and the black man I turned away the other night continued to haunt me. The man had been so desperate trying not to fall through the cracks, and I felt I pushed him over the edge. Why did he have to come in for assistance during a rule change? I hoped that maybe he would come back.

When I was preparing to begin work, I looked up from my table and saw a tall, thin, Spanish man somewhere in his thirties with a pale complexion standing in the doorway. He was smartly dressed in a black suit covered by a full length, unbuttoned black leather coat giving him the appearance of a European. I couldn't figure how he had gotten downstairs, unless he was bold enough to just walk by our guard, or maybe the guard was afraid to stop him. No one had noticed, so I went over to question him. He said he had waited hours, days, and couldn't get ahead of the Asian population. I asked him where he lived and he replied, "The Red Zone". I felt sorry and told him I would do his case, but I'd have to angle to get him in because I didn't want to cause a riot outside. There was another young man with him who stood in the background and never uttered a word. No one was seeing clients for another five minutes, and so rather than turn them away I took him and his partner to my table.

The shyer of the two men was away on business and saw the incident on television. His partner was in the apartment sleeping when he heard the first plane. When it hit, his entire building shook and shuddered. He flew out of bed, grabbed a few personal effects, and ran for the lobby. When the second plane hit, he was waiting in the lobby trying to get some information as to what exactly was happening. Several of the tenants decided to get out of the building so, he too left, and shortly after the Towers began to collapse. He was asthmatic and managed to stay away from the tidal wave of black, all-engulfing dust that chased him and tried to swallow his entire being. He was terrified, and as he told the story he was having difficulty breathing. I asked him if he wanted to see the nurse, but he declined and continued the story. During the attack all the dust and debris stormed their open windows, destroying the contents of their apartment. They brought in documentation stating that they couldn't return to their residence until perhaps after December 1 because of the danger and the fact that it was a crime scene. They had been let in briefly twice since the incident. The first time they went in to survey the damage, and the second trip was with an insurance adjuster. After 9/11, they started using all of their savings to pay for food, hotels, and daily needs. They had run out of money and had come to us for assistance. They stated that they were depressed and felt so hopeless.

Because the men were living near Ground Zero and were entitled to benefits, they received a check from FEMA for $2000 and had paid part of their rent with it. I wrote disbursing orders for clothing, reimbursement for their hotel, food, Family Maintenance Plan, and their utilities.

When I brought my paperwork before the supervisor, they said things had changed again. I would have to get FEMA to extend rental payments. I could only give the client disbursing orders for food for $100 and the Family Maintenance Grant for $250, and I knew with just that they weren't going to make it. I telephoned FEMA and after quite awhile I got them to agree to take care of the rent indefinitely, so one problem was solved. I advocated for the clients, hoping to get them more assistance. The coordinator's response to my efforts was to tell me I was too stressed, and as soon as the clients left, I was to go speak with mental health. In this case, it wasn't stress with me; I was pissed off. I couldn't imagine how it would be to try and run an operation when the rules were changing every day. It was frustrating our caseworkers and clients to the breaking point.

Another change came down from headquarters. We had to call in everything except food and family maintenance allowance via the telephone to headquarters. It was slowing everything down creating more tension and longer lines outside the door. It was an almost impossible situation and my mantra became: Flexible, Flexible, Flexible.

So, after not being able to give my clients what I thought they needed, I went to mental health. Many mental health workers were skilled professionals and very valuable to our teams, but when a person sits in front of you and tells you how you feel and what you are thinking, it is a bit much. I just agreed with her and was about to go on my way when she told me to take the day off because I wasn't going to be of any use to the clients. I went back to work anyway. She spent the rest of her day either sitting at my table, or watching me from her table. I did very well with my clients; it wasn't the clients who were the problem. I was an advocate for my clients no matter what the price and if it meant that I had to go see mental health, so be it. Normally, mental health was very sympathetic with the caseworkers that fought for the clients and often had wonderful suggestions to help with their causes. I had just gotten an inexperienced person who didn't have a clue.

The rest of the day, I had four Chinese garment workers and the interesting point was they were all married to men many years their senior. The men were unemployed and sat in front of me with vacant stares and disgusting yellow teeth. I wished I could have spoken with the women because they all seemed to be so afraid. Even our mental health workers couldn't assist them; they couldn't communicate in the same language. It was exasperating.

The day finally came to a close and the mental health worker gave up on watching me work. She finally zoomed in on another caseworker and succeeded in making the worker angry. I smiled at her as I left, thanking God she was out of my face. I wanted to be alone. After seeing clients non-stop and being involved in the politics of the job I needed some personal space. The walk to the subway was quiet and I was glad the day had ended as I began to think about dinner at Joe G's. When I arrived at Park Central I immediately got into different clothing and walked to the restaurant where I enjoyed a couple of Manhattans, a good dinner, and a warm greeting from the staff.

24 October 2001 – Wednesday
Lower Manhattan, New York

In the early morning I received a phone call telling me to report to headquarters to become part of a "Hot Shot" team. Thanks be to God I was away from the smell of those toilets. The team required that we as a small group were to go directly to the apartments of the people who weren't going into the service center for one reason on another. Some people had begun to return to their apartments and then of course, there were the people who didn't evacuate when ordered. We went back to the outreach routine, except we were going to specific addresses. The teams were scattered all over the boroughs because people had moved in every direction. Our particular clients were located in lower Manhattan inside the Red and Yellow zones, which we thought would make our job easier by not requiring us to travel very far. After I met my new teammates, we were off on the Metro for the day to complete our assignments. We were carrying disbursing orders, which meant that we had to return to the headquarters in Brooklyn again at night to check them back into Records and Reports, which gave us a long tiring day.

There were four of us, Maria the nurse, Janet the mental health worker, and Paul and me, the two family service workers. Our first and most interesting case was calling on a woman whom the neighbors said had not left her apartment since September 11. We arrived at an apartment building, just south of Canal Street. It was chaos, with the tenants' hand carrying out their possessions, breaking leases and leaving. We were back in our Red Cross work vests and we clearly stood out. The tenants smiled at us and said things like: "God Bless you for your work." "Thanks so much for the help." "Be safe."

It was an expensive place with a luxurious lobby complete with a doorman in uniform. We spoke to him and he told us the floor on which to find the woman, wished us luck and told us to be careful. We tried to phone her first, but she didn't respond, so we took the elevator to her apartment on the twenty-second floor. When we knocked, an older Hungarian woman opened the door and peered through three chains, and when we told her who we were she started to cry. The mental health worker, Janet, convinced her to open the door by explaining that we were from the Red Cross and we had come to be of assistance to her. After she saw our identification she invited us into an apartment that stank of cats, cigarettes, and stale beer. Her unwashed light brown hair hung in strings over the collar of her torn blue silk flowered bathrobe that resembled a wallpaper pattern. The attacks had traumatized her, and it appeared she was drowning her fears and insecurities in alcohol. We didn't know if she had a previous problem, but if she did the attack had intensified it. She told us it was going to happen again, and we were all going to die, and we should leave New York as soon as possible. She stated that she was never going outside again, at which Janet took over. I wrote her disbursing orders to meet her immediate needs, while the woman and Janet went into the kitchen for privacy; we sat and waited. I had white cat hair all over my black jeans and Maria the nurse began to sneeze. The woman had sealed up all her windows with plastic and tape so no "bad" air could get into the apartment. She did that after the attack and had locked in all sorts of toxic dusts from the explosions. It was difficult to breathe in her home. The other family service worker Paul made arrangements to get the apartment cleaned, and our mental health worker did a great job convincing the woman that we would all survive, and that she had to get on with her life. The woman who had opened the door looked like a different person when we left. She was more relaxed and talked about stocking up on groceries with the disbursing order we gave her, which meant she was going outside. I felt good and realized that we had made a difference in someone's life, and that, after all, was why we were out here in the first place.

We called on four other people, mostly cases that Maria needed to handle. We wrote disbursing orders and enjoyed meeting and assisting the clients. Our cases were time consuming and we didn't stop for lunch, which left us all with noisy stomachs. We wanted to finish before dark because we knew we had to take the Metro back to Brooklyn and then back to Times Square. If we finished at a decent hour, we would stop for dinner. Some nights it was so late that I was too tired to eat, and just wanted to get back to go to sleep.

We did stop as a group at an all-too expensive diner where we indulged in Indian cuisine. The food wasn't that good, but it was nice to be done for the day and eat with friends. My experiences with teams were the longer I worked on one the tighter we would grow. It became like family because we depended on each other, our jobs intertwined, and we were always concerned about the other members' welfare.

25 October 2001 – Thursday
Lower Manhattan, New York

I was beginning to feel like an empty jug of water. I had given so much of myself away that there wasn't anything left. I was extremely tired both mentally and physically. I thought I might be coming down with pneumonia. It was difficult to take a deep breath and my chest hurt from coughing. I didn't go to nursing because I knew I was leaving for home soon where I would see my own physician. I didn't have a fever and other than the bronchial problem, I felt physically good just a bit exhausted. My mental state was another issue. I was being plagued by nightmares and had developed a startle response to loud or sudden noises.

We started out early in the same team from Brooklyn back onto the Metro. Before we entered the Zone, Paul, the other caseworker, asked a group of police officers if he could snap their picture. There were six of them and the officer said, "No," and took his camera. He looked so shocked. The officer laughed and told us to join the group of NYPD. He took our picture with Paul's camera and then one of the officers pulled out a small pocket-sized camera and took another. "You guys got a picture with the NYPD to take back home, and we got a picture of a Red Cross team," he said as they all laughed. Light moments like that helped us get through tough days.

In lower Manhattan, the buildings were so tall they seemed to touch the clouds, and the streets were so narrow that they never allowed us to see the sun unless it was straight overhead. There was usually a freezing wind passing all around the shops and apartments. When we were inside the apartments, we could hear the wind beating on the windows, always howling like a mournful ghost.

Working on a "Hot Shot" team always required miles of walking and climbing stairs, searching for addresses and information. We talked to many people and everyone questioned us, as if we were the EPA. They were all terrified about what they were breathing. No one questioned my cough because many of the clients had the same complaint.

We went to visit a client who had just re-occupied his apartment and was suffering from stress and acute asthma. We had visited him previously, and he only needed assistance from our medical team. When they went upstairs the manager came over to talk with Paul and me as we waited in the lobby. He told us a story of an experience he had had, which was sad, but had a touch of humor to it.

According to the manager there was a mass evacuation of the neighborhood, including his building. Pets were deserted and tenants were hysterical, especially a young Russian woman who was very attached to her tiny black and white terrier, Clitch. It was four days before she finally had the opportunity to rescue the dog, but when she got into her apartment Clitch was gone. The authorities had allotted a four hour time period for the residents to enter the Zone to check out their apartments, and get their belongings. But because she couldn't find the dog she wouldn't leave, and proceeded to bang on doors, screaming that one of the neighbors had stolen Glitch. The manager removed his navy blue cap and ran his fingers through his thick black hair, and told us the soldiers had escorted her back to the other side of the barricades. The military wouldn't tolerate her erratic behavior, so the Zone was off limits to her. The manager with his sad eyes was searching for something that could add humor to tragedy, and maybe even possibly lighten our load. He was a kind man and he smiled and persisted.

A neighbor had found the dog, and in turn was evacuated herself, but couldn't catch Glitch, so she left him behind. The pampered little animal was to fend for himself in the apartment.

At first, the Russian woman almost started a riot going to the police at the barricades telling them she had to return because her baby was in the apartment, until they realized she was talking about a pet. The unbalanced, petite woman walked the barrier lines driving the police and soldiers to the breaking point, insisting with great tenacity that they let her back in to recover her dog. They wouldn't, even though she nagged, whined, begged, and pleaded. As a last resort, she began to bug him, as he was the manager of the apartments. He went to the police and soldiers at the barricade, and when they realized that he was the manager of the building that the woman who was driving them all nuts lived in, they let him in just to get the dog. The other woman, who had rescued the terrier, notified him as to what happened to the animal, and that she suspected the dog was still running around her apartment. He wondered why she hadn't brought the dog out with her. As he mumbled to himself in Italian that his job was not that of a dogcatcher, he rode to the building within the Yellow Zone on his Vespa. He parked the vehicle and entered the apartment building. He dragged his heavy body up flights of stairs, and used his passkey to enter the unit. The insidious odor overwhelmed him the minute he stepped inside. The black and white spotted dog had pooped everywhere, and had torn up the couch dragging cotton fill to each room. Then the monstrous little animal had gone to the bathroom looking for water in the toilet. From there he began to play with the toilet paper and had dragged it from room to room until he reached the end of the roll. The dog was quick and the manager couldn't catch him. He chased Glitch all over the unit falling over the furniture, climbing on the bed and crawling under the kitchen table bumping his head, until he finally trapped the little beast in the bedroom and threw a blanket over him. He proceeded to stuff Glitch into a large carry-on made of a heavy red carpet material. The exhausted and out of breath manager hurried down flights of stairs, as Glitch snapped and bit at the inside of the large bag. When he reached the street, he slung the carrier over the handlebars of his Vespa. It threw him off balance and gave the older man the appearance of being a drunk driver, as his motor scooter moved toward the barricade. When he neared the barrier, all the police officers, and soldiers removed their hats and applauded. The manager told us he was a sight because he had torn his coat and had a huge bump on his head. Also, the dog had bitten his hand and he had blood on his shirt and face. The waiting Russian woman grabbed the carry-on without so much as a thank-you, talking to the dog like a returned, kidnapped child, and immediately releasing him from the red carpet bag. She threw the soldiers and the police a nasty look, flipped her black hair over her shoulder, turned and walked away. Everyone was glad to see her and her dog disappear down the windy Manhattan Street. They all hoped they would never see her again. I looked at the manager and wondered if this story was true, or whether he was just trying to bring a smile to the faces of two weary disaster relief workers.

The medical team, Maria and Janet, returned to the lobby and we were ready for our last visit of the day. We said goodbye to the manager and thanked him for being so kind to us. We had done six cases, which was excellent, considering the time we had spent on each. As we were leaving Maria said, "Did you see the manager's hand? Was he bitten by a dog?"

We took the Metro to a residence just inside the south of Canal Street border, which was still in the Yellow Zone. The woman we were to visit lived in a loft on the top floor of an old brick building that stood alone. It was a giant sentinel standing by itself like a lost child in a neighborhood full of what once must have been factories. An iron fire escape zigzagged up the dirty brick façade like a massive parasite clinging to its only nourishment. When we rang the bell, and entered, the woman yelled from above that the elevator was broken, and to take the stairs – all twelve flights. All I could see was her long straight brown hair hanging down over her face as she leaned over the banister and called to us. We looked at the purple walls as we trudged up the blue wooden stairs. A couple of brown rats scurried across the stairs and disappeared somewhere into a large crack in the wall that connected to the staircase. On the walls from floor to ceiling painted circles as big as dinner plates stared out at us and in the center of each circle was a photograph of a head. Twisted around the banister going up to the woman's apartment were white Christmas lights giving the illusion of delicate cobwebs and reflecting a gentle glow on the stairs.

Finally, out of breath and ready to collapse we reached the top. Our heavy-set nurse, Maria had four more flights to go. After the first two flights, she had slowed down, stopping occasionally to sit for a moment before climbing again. I shook the waiting woman's hand and entered her home. Black and white photographs of people, mostly children, covered every wall. The young woman invited us to sit in her brown wicker chairs in the spacious book-filled loft. I reached over and moved an enormous calico cat off of the rocking chair and sat down. I was fascinated because her entire house was one enormous room. I asked her how we could be of assistance to her and she told us how angry she was at the Red Cross. She felt Red Cross had unjustly treated her friend and she wanted to air her complaints with Paul and me.

She told me that when the buildings collapsed her friend had run toward them to find his daughter who worked there. He was hit, grazed by falling debris, and was taken to the hospital where he was treated and immediately released. The photographer had heard that the injured were getting a great deal of money, but her friend hadn't received anything. She was gearing up for a fight. I told her hospitalization overnight was required to receive benefits, but asked her to tell me the rest of the story.

She sensed our concern was sincere and she calmed down. The woman told me the man informed the authorities that his daughter who had been working that morning at an insurance company in the Towers was missing. He posted missing fliers with her picture and his phone number. "Please call me if you have seen Suzanne. She is missing as of 9/11. My family has fallen apart." They had not found the body and he didn't know what to do, so he withdrew from everyone. It was too painful for him to discuss, so he didn't seek any further help.

I informed the photographer about the enormous amount of benefits that her friend was entitled to and had not received. Her ears perked up and she apologized for biting my head off, and offered us a cup of tea. The nurse was sitting on the landing of the eighth flight of stairs, still the color of the wall and out of breath, and the mental health worker hadn't even attempted the stairs, so it was just the two family service workers and the photographer. We had our tea and, as we talked to her, she began to understand our genuine concern. We told her we would contact her friend. She was pleased with our caring and willingness to follow up on the man. She said she was unable to go to the center, but needed assistance too. She was having breathing problems and her business had collapsed because the clients couldn't get past the barriers. She said until the incident she had never had a health problem. We told her she was eligible for assistance and I wrote out some disbursing orders to give her a needed helping hand. I filled out a form for her to pick up an air purifier that hopefully would help clean the air in the loft. It was a difficult visit listening to the terrible pain and anger she had harbored through a misunderstanding. The photographer was under extreme stress and didn't need any more put upon her. She saw us out and told us to be careful. All throughout the Zone I had come to hear over and over again the salutation, "Be safe – Be careful". It was almost like at home when everyone says, "Have a good day", except there were no more good days.

It was getting dark as we headed for the subway. It had been a long day and I was tired. At headquarters we checked in our disbursing orders. We were informed that tomorrow we would be on a different "Hot Shot" team. I was getting used to the constant changes and didn't care. I left headquarters and caught the "A" train back to Lincoln Circle in midtown Manhattan and walked to Joe G's for a quiet dinner, after which I returned to the hotel for the night. I no longer slept all night with nightmares dancing through my tired brain. I would wake up at all hours shaking because the dreams seemed so real.

26 October 2001 – Friday
Lower Manhattan, New York

We became a new team of three, the mental health worker, Janet; Paul and me, for Family Services. Our team nurse Maria had left, so we were short one important member. Her blood pressure had become an issue and she was suffering from exhaustion and was sent home.

We had an address to visit in a building that was in sight of the Trade Center. I couldn't believe anyone was living there. Why weren't the people in the building evacuated? Most had left under their own volition, but some had stayed. It was a huge, dirty building with a segment of low-income apartments laced throughout. The building didn't have a doorman, or any security that we could see.

We went to visit with an elderly disabled lady whose neighbors had called Red Cross informing us that she was in need of assistance. The halls were a hospital green and dirt covered the torn rugs. The elevator was a box full of mirrors, with only a rack of buttons and an emergency phone. It smelled of urine. It lurched and groaned on its journey to the 26th floor. The apartment we were looking for was at the end of a dark, narrow hallway. We knocked on a steel door and heard a loud voice from the inside call to us; "Come on in." We identified ourselves, opened the front door, and stepped into a small, clean and sunny apartment. Sitting in the corner by the large aluminum-framed window was an old white woman with huge, swollen legs wrapped in yards of support bandages. She couldn't walk to the door because her legs would no longer support her horrendous weight. She had on a worn pink chenille bathrobe that hugged her husky body with a pack of Camels peeking out of the pocket. Her hair was a snowy field of pin curls wrapped in a colorful bandana. She was delighted for any company, as she spent her days alone sitting in her chair. When you looked out her windows the entire site was easy to view. She had a small balcony where mops and brooms were stored. It was several inches deep in asbestos and cement dust. The wind whistled through her windows like haunting voices screaming from the depths of the Trade Center. She was a pleasant woman, sitting on several large pillows, just feet from the television, the telephone, and a box of Depend adult diapers. She told us that a woman came in to help her every afternoon, but lately she hadn't shown up because she was afraid of the air quality. Her neighbor was making her a meal every day and helping her get into bed at night. She related the frightening story about the day it happened and what she saw.

She was sitting in her chair gazing out the window when the first plane crashed into the Tower. She was petrified with fear, but thought it was an accident. When the second one hit, she knew it wasn't. She said she began to pray and was prepared to die. When the buildings fell she was afraid that one of the buildings was going to fall on her 26th floor apartment. She suffered from asthma and a heart condition, and I was amazed that the shock of what she saw hadn't killed her. We sat in her sun-filled room on a couch that had handmade lace dollies on the arms and fancy pillows at each end. The old widow woman was so alone. We talked a long time and she showed us pictures from many years ago of her wedding in Romania, and her children, who were no longer living. The woman existed on a small pension, and received assistance from the government on her rent. The day of the incident her next door neighbors had helped get the old woman downstairs and out of the area. After a few days, she returned to her unit and said she was more comfortable being home, but could we have someone clean her apartment and her balcony. They were covered with the deadly dust that was everywhere in the Zone. We explained that we would have someone assist her with that. Paul wrote disbursing orders for various needs, such as food, reimbursement of hotel expenses, payment of utilities, and the family grant. Janet read them over checking for errors and, finding none, handed them back to Paul who explained them to the old woman. The woman was grateful for our help and told us we had relieved her of many worries. As we were leaving, I leaned down to hug her; she reached up and put her hands on both sides of my face and whispered in my ear, "You are the angels I have prayed for. May God protect you."

We took the metro to our next assignment, which was just south of Canal Street in an old apartment building. We nearly froze to death walking from the subway to the apartment. But the building was warm and inviting when we entered. We had the address of another client, but the uniformed doorman refused to ring the woman's apartment. "Hey, she's a nut. You sure you wanna go up there?" I told the doorman that it was our job to visit the woman, but if he didn't want to ring her that was okay. He said, "Whatever. I'm just warning you." His Brooklyn accent was so thick that I had to listen carefully in order to understand him. We thanked him as we got into the elevator. He shrugged his shoulders, threw his hands up in the air, and walked back to the front desk.

We went up to the 33rd floor and down a narrow hall until we came to a door with handwritten signs all over it – "Do Not Enter without a Respirator. Beware! Look What the Government Has Done to Us. This apartment is bugged by the FBI." Bracing for the worst, Paul knocked on the door, which quickly opened just a crack. "We are from the Red Cross, and we were told you were in need of assistance",

Paul piped out in his most polite voice. "You're not from the goddamn government are you?" came the strained female voice from within the apartment. We assured her we were not a government organization, at which she opened the door and invited us in. She was a pitifully thin, blonde woman who didn't stand five feet tall. She had a large black mongrel dog. She stood there glaring at us as the dog sniffed our clothing. The apartment was a collection of years of junk piled to the ceiling leaving only a small path through the rooms for the woman and her dog. The client had collected newspapers, rags, magazines, books, clothing, rolled-up rugs, and multitudes of boxes with mysterious contents. We barely fit in the main room. The woman immediately began to talk, and went on and on, quickly throwing her words at us like bullets. She snapped out to me, "The goddamn landlord wouldn't fix the goddamn broken window and all the dust blew in here from the explosion. It's all a plot by the government you know." Paul sat on the floor and Janet, in her arrogance sat on the only chair, while I propped myself up on a pile of oriental rugs that was covered with a strange dust that hurt when I breathed. We quietly waited for her to finish raving. The mentally unbalanced woman sat on the floor demanding, demanding, and complaining as she chewed on her fingernails. She had a small pillbox hat on with a short black veil over her face exposing her green eyes, and an old stripped rayon blue dress that was worn out and hung like a rag on her emaciated body. As I listened I looked at her bare feet and my heart went out to her. From whatever demon the woman was suffering, it was going to be our job to try and relieve some of her stress. She shook, and reached for her dog, twisting his long curly hair as she began to communicate with us. Paul and I patiently explained the Red Cross assistance available to her. The woman had never heard of us, and Janet was useless in helping us explain who we were. Janet would make faces at the woman every time she wasn't looking. I was appalled at such unprofessional behavior. Under her breath I heard her whisper the word, "Crone". I couldn't believe it and hoped the old woman didn't hear her cruel remark. Paul was shocked at the condition of the apartment but it wasn't anything he hadn't seen before, and being the pro that he was he didn't show any reaction to the situation other than patience and kindness. I petted the dog, which slobbered all over me, and tried to calm the woman down enough that we could help her. I had to go out in the apartment house hallway to write the disbursing orders. I laid my paperwork out on the floor of the hall where at least there was room to work. I paid a month's rent, gave her food, a Family Maintenance Grant, and tried to give her references to other agencies. She objected, yelled and carried on and on. She said if we gave her name to another agency, they would send someone to kill her. I thought Janet would intervene, but she didn't. Finally, I just had to make the old lady stop. We did everything we could for her, and as we left the apartment the woman reached out and patted Paul on the back and gave me a quick smile. When Janet went out the door the old woman gave her the finger. The woman might have been mentally ill, but she was no fool, and she knew that Janet treated her with disrespect. We left on a somewhat good note and went to the bathroom in the lobby and washed up and blew our noses in an attempt to clean out the molds, dusts, and asbestos. Janet was horrified at the client and the living conditions. I assumed that she was inexperienced and had not been exposed to the environments that Paul and I had. It was not difficult for us to accept people for who they were and we were not bothered by where they chose to live, or by the abuse they threw at us. We had a job to do and I felt we were good at it. No matter how tired I was I always had more energy for the clients.

After leaving the apartment building we went to a Puerto Rican restaurant just north of Canal Street where I found a comfortable, private booth and went over all my paperwork. I wanted everything in good order when I returned to Brooklyn. Sitting in the restaurant, I began to think how much I wanted to include real stainless flatware in my life again. Maybe that was one of the features of Joe G's that made me so comfortable. Everyday I was eating off of plastic forks, paper plates, and drinking from Styrofoam cups. The food in the restaurant was nothing to rave about, but it was adequate. The time was slipping through our fingers, so we decided to do one more case before packing it in for the day. Our cases had taken more time than we had planned, but that happened sometimes and there wasn't much we could do about it.

We took the subway into Chinatown and went to two addresses where the residents didn't speak any English. We didn't have an interpreter, so we had to leave. Often, if we went to a residence of a foreign person the children living there acted as interpreters. In these two cases, both families were elderly and we couldn't find an available interpreter. We would have someone go out the next day to take the two calls for us. I was glad to leave after being greeted by several large rats in the hallways. We're talking rats as big as cats. We stamped around and were noisy and they scurried away after glaring at us for what seemed like forever, bringing back to me childhood memories of the aggressive rats that threatened us in the cold water flat we lived in in San Francisco. As we left there I gave a thought to my fears. However, our determination to help the people overrode the fear. Without that determination I don't think any of us could have continued on this job.

I was anxious for the day to end because in the morning I had to go through the out-processing at headquarters and then would be heading home at last. So, we called it a day, having done all of our paperwork. We went back to Brooklyn to check in our disbursing orders. My team asked me out to dinner, but, I declined. I went back to the hotel and spent a fitful night fighting off nightmares. My cases, the smells, the tragedy kept running through my mind like I had pressed the rewind button on a video player.

27 October 2001 – Saturday
Brooklyn – Manhattan, New York

I got up at 4:30 a.m. and took a shower. I caught the 6:30 a.m. bus to headquarters for out-processing. Headquarters was doing a booming business with new volunteers coming in every hour. The people on the bus lined up outside to be checked by the security guards, who performed their usual searches before the workers were allowed to enter the building. The coordinator spotted me, pulled me aside asked me to extend my stay, and I thought, *"You want blood?"* I was worn out and felt that I had given my absolute all. There was no more to give.

It was required that various functions sign my check-out sheet for me to leave the job. First, I went to the Logistics office. They were the people in charge of the cars and telephones. I didn't have either, so I cleared there quickly. The man in charge said to me, "Sweetie you are all gray. Do you feel okay?" He was very concerned, but I thought I looked fine. For God's sake I had clean clothes on and didn't smell like death. He wanted my identification badge. I asked him if there was anyway I could keep it. He saw the green stripe and knew I was a Ground Zero worker. He said, "Small thing to ask. Let me stamp it void and then I will forget you have it." I thanked him. I knew the badge was a piece of history and I wanted to frame it. From that office, I went to nursing and waited for twenty minutes. I sat on a long wooden bench with another worker, who was engrossed in the New York Times. All I could see behind his paper was the top of his bald head.

When it was my turn I entered the nursing office, and the elderly nurse told me to take a seat. I sat down in front of her table in a folding chair. She said, "How are you?" I wasn't doing that well and insisted that she document my bronchial problem. She wrote it down, and gave me a tube of cough drops. She asked me where I had been working because family service workers were in many locations. When I told her, she sighed deeply, checked off my sheet, and said, "Dear, when you go home, go to your doctor and get a base line x-ray. No telling what all those carcinogenic materials you inhaled are going to do to you down the line." That was a cheerful thought, with my aching lungs and horrendous cough. Then I went upstairs to the mental health office. A young woman took me out in a busy hall and said, "How was the job?" People were walking by, so I smiled and said I really didn't feel I could discuss it. She gave me a teddy bear, checked me off, and told me to have a safe flight home. Technically, I was not debriefed and would later pay dearly for the careless move on the part of that mental health worker. I cleared accounting in ten minutes and then proceeded to staffing, which was my last stop. Staffing checked my papers and released me.

I took the subway back to Manhattan, and realized I had most of the day to myself. I had to do something in New York beside work, so I decided to go to a play. I had never been to a play and it was a new and exciting experience. I walked to a nearby theater on Broadway and bought a ticket to the afternoon performance. I showed the man in the ticket office my Red Cross identification and he sold me a ticket for $25, which was unbelievably reasonable. The ticket was stamped, "HERO". (That label of Hero was to stick on me like a parasite in the future months. My work itself evoked nothing for me but pain and sadness.) The ticket salesman was so courteous thanking me for working in New York, which I really appreciated. My seat to see *The Proof* with Jennifer Jason Leigh was fourth row center. I walked back to the hotel, packed my luggage, and returned to the theater in the afternoon.

The Walter Kerr Theater in midtown Manhattan was smaller than the average modern arts center, but elegant murals graced the walls with a Renaissance theme. There were red velvet curtains draped from the sidewalls, and fresco type paintings on the ceilings. The set on stage was that of the exterior of an old house. It looked as if someone had taken a house and deposited it onto the stage. The inside of the theater was cold. I had my Red Cross sweatshirt on because it was the only warm thing I had brought to New York beside the black coat I had purchased, and the sweater I bought with Sara that didn't fit. Before the play began, the people on both sides of me kept firing questions about the Red Cross at me. I went there to get away, which didn't work, but I liked the people and talked to them. They were looking for information from some source other than the media. One of the men was from San Francisco, but had moved to New York for his business, and the other was a teacher at the University of California Berkeley. It was strange that all three of us were from California – small world.

I particularly liked Jennifer Jason Leigh as a movie actress, and in the play she was great. I never realized how loud the participants had to speak. There were only four people in the entire play, but it worked very well. I missed the middle part because I fell asleep. After the play I walked back to the hotel. The weather had turned hot and muggy, so I took my time looking in the air-conditioned shops where I bought a couple of lightweight shirts. When I was paying for my purchase the merchant told his friend that the authorities had found six more bodies that morning, and that the barricade was moved back from Chambers Street. I wondered how long they would be finding bodies and body parts. It was all so depressing. I thought perhaps it would be the last time I would ever be in Times Square. I liked New York, with its great energy and even its sadness.

Upon returning to the hotel I took a shower, and then went to Joe G's to eat a substantial dinner, and said goodbye to the bartender and the waiter who had been so kind to me. I could hardly stay awake through my dinner.

28 October 2001 – Sunday
Manhattan, New York
GOING HOME!

I got up early and took a long walk over to St. Patrick's to pray for a safe journey. I walked in on a Communion service, which couldn't have been better. After the service, I hurried back to the hotel because I had to catch the airport shuttle at 11:10 a.m. I did a double check on my room to make sure I had gotten everything and then I went downstairs juggling my two suitcases, a carry-on, my photo portfolio, my lunch bag, and my purse when my cell phone rang. It was my Chapter telling me something about a poster. I really had no idea what they were talking about. I couldn't help them, and told them I was on my way home. The worker wished me a safe journey and said she was anxious to see me. Contact with home always felt so great. The ride to JFK airport took a long time, a long way from Times Square.

When I arrived at the airport I dragged my suitcases to the main door. Right inside of the door was a luggage x-ray machine for all of the bags. I had to pick up my big bag along with the small one and put them on the conveyor belt. It was interesting because it was the first time I had to pass my big bag through such a device. They probed and checked and said okay, at which I proceeded to the ticket counter to get my electronic one-way ticket. Having extended my stay required changing my original ticket. I waited about twenty minutes until my ticket was issued. The clerk said, "We're gonna search you. Please step aside." It was as if I had won a prize. I again dragged all my bags, my lunch, my photo portfolio, and my purse over to a big table. They made me open the bags and went through everything. They even put a bomb probe into my lunch bag, and then physically searched me. I understood that security had to be tight, but the people checking the bags were rude. It would've lightened it up had they been polite. There were armed soldiers and police present, but I must say I was getting used to them. When they finished, they told me to go down a long corridor to the Delta waiting lounge, as they took my big bag away to the land of luggage, hopefully somewhere in the belly of the correct airplane.

I went to the USO. It was such a wonderful respite and the environment was quiet. I stayed there for an hour, hunkered down on a big, soft sofa, and watched television. When it came time to board my Delta flight, each person had to show two identification cards. I had a passport, a Red Cross ID, and a current military card along with a California Driver's License. There were seven passengers searched and I was one of them. Security took everything out of my carry-on with little concern for breakage. The woman was bored with her job, rough with the luggage, and rude to me. I didn't see the point in searching the same bag over and over again. I didn't understand why the airport wasn't profiling people instead of picking individuals at random. If only seven bags and passengers were checked, what did the other passengers have in their bags and on their persons?

The security woman said she would confiscate anything sharp, as if I were stupid enough to carry a sharp object. Of course, I didn't say anything. Then she searched my photo portfolio, and then she searched me again. Of course, I was metal sensitive with blue jeans and metal all over my clothing. As the episode continued, the clerk got ruder and ruder. She took my journal manuscripts, a page at a time, and shook them out. Finally, she told me to empty my pockets, at which I tossed a rosary and some Red Cross pins onto a tray. At that point, she told me to board the plane. I was the last person to board and they were waiting for me. I had been through a police state check. I felt violated, especially when she manhandled my manuscripts.

I was a frequent flyer and never had any fear. I preferred flying to any other mode of transportation. Nevertheless I kept seeing in my mind's eye the plane becoming a missile and I was nervous. I quietly started to cry behind my sunglasses, so I decided to distract myself and rent the movie on board. I gave the flight attendant $5.00, took the headset, sat back and waited for my nonstop flight to take off. The flight attendant returned my money, and thanked me for coming to New York and said everything on the plane was free to any Red Cross worker.

I always reacted to disaster with nerves of steel having a first responder personality, but when it was over I often suffered. I had seen and heard too much and wasn't walking away free from New York. I was going home with bronchitis and a case of post-traumatic stress.

A girl from Columbia University sat next to me as people began to move around after take-off. The plane was only about twenty-percent full, so we had choices of seats. She was going home to visit her parents in San Francisco. Her name was Jackie, and the fragrance of roses spilled over her tan linen jumper and chic blonde hair. She spotted my Red Cross sweat shirt and wanted to talk. Jackie was worried because she was grinding her teeth, and having re-occurring nightmares and thought she might be developing a mental illness. The young woman said that she didn't know what was real anymore. It had to be a bad dream and it had to end. She had lost a friend in the incident. At night she created missing persons posters and tacked them up all over Manhattan every morning, but she heard nothing. In desperation she decided to get as far away as possible from the entire scene and was taking this flight to San Francisco. All the stories were but tentacles spreading over the entire country, tragedy seeping like a poison into our personal security. I gave her some printed material that nursing had given me on response to disaster and grief. We talked for about an hour and I was glad I was able to help her. So many people were suffering and couldn't make any sense out of what had happened, or understand the terrible impact of change we were all enduring.

Molly, the flight attendant, was the next to sit down with me. She asked me for an autograph and to be her pen friend. I asked her what I did to merit that. She said the Red Cross was so brave that she felt it an honor to talk to any of us. I told her I was just doing the job that I had been trained to do, and was glad I had been sent.

She was having a rough time flying with what happened to the crews of American Airlines Flight 11 and United Airlines Flight 175. As she spoke her soft brown eyes filled with tears and her satin skin took on a reddish hue. We shared our anxieties, and she sat with me off and on over the entire flight. I think we were a comfort to each other.

After an uneventful flight, I arrived battle-worn and tired in San Francisco. It wasn't a good scene, with armed soldiers, FBI, detectives, and police everywhere. I retrieved my bags and went to the Airporter Express outside, only to discover it had changed its schedule to every two hours after 6:00 p.m. I had to wait until 8:00 p.m. to finally get the bus. There were fewer flights, less customers, and it no longer profited the bus company to run every hour. I became acutely aware that our lives would never be the same again and that in protecting our freedom we would be losing some of it. I felt I had stepped over a line and that there was no going back for me. My life was radically changed

THE RETURN
Falls Church, Virginia - New York, New York

Redeployed in December of 2001, I worked in a huge unmarked warehouse in Falls Church, Virginia on a hotline regarding 9/11 where I supervised a Red Cross casework team of eight. The Red Cross had mostly employed what seemed to me to be about one-hundred temporary hires from a local agency to do most of the work. The warehouse had no windows and hundreds of computers in long rows. One of the coordinators told me the building was the length of a football field. We worked long hours in that windowless building with its low ceilings. We didn't see the clients and did all our work through the phones and the computers. We received calls from all over the country. I was there two weeks. Then the Red Cross flew me back to Ground Zero where I worked as an outreach Family Service team supervisor in January and February 2002. The wonderful resilience of the city was visible in the tremendous effort on the part of the people to return to normal. Unfortunately, some buildings had lost their structural integrity and their futures were doubtful. Crews still dug at the "pile" for bodies or parts. The search extended to nearby buildings, and the pain had not left the eyes of the people, but they were the toughest individuals I had ever met and I knew one day it would be but an agonizing part of their history. I respected them and considered it a privilege to return to work with them again. I still had a serious cough, seemingly impossible to shake, and post-traumatic stress had set in, but that wasn't to become a problem for at least a year. My own recovery efforts reminded me every day of the struggles of the people in New York. Returning to work there I felt less isolated than being home in California.

Unfortunately, after leaving this job I worked non-stop for four years on fifteen disasters responses all over the United States and as far away as Guam. One of my responses required me to live in the disaster zone for five months working a long term recovery job. I couldn't stop running because it deadened the emotional pain I was enduring. When home between jobs I met a stranger, Paul Lane, at Mass one Sunday who told me about a retreat for first responders in Inverness, California. In June 2005, I spent five days at the West Coast Post-Trauma retreat, intensely trying to deal with post-traumatic stress and my own exhaustion. They helped me put my life on a better track, slowing me down long enough to face the pain and to try to understand it. I have since then come to realize that Red Cross was but a channel for my humanitarian work, and now volunteer as a liaison in a hospital emergency room, which is a trauma center. I no longer travel with the disaster team, but use my incredible experience and skills still working one-on-one with wounded people. The experience of 9/11 robbed me of any feeling that my life was safe. I also now work as a volunteer for the police on a patrol team and as a Crime Victims' Advocate. I want to continue my humanitarian work, and being with the police I may be able to play some small role in making my community safe, so people won't have to endure the feelings we all acquired at Ground Zero. We all left 9/11, never to look at anything the same again, understanding the preciousness and fragility of human life. We who worked there in any capacity continue to heal and struggle with the pain of our experiences surrounding that September morning and will for a very long time to come. I return to New York City twice a year at Christmas and September 11th to the site, trying still to understand why it all happened. I have not been able to grasp that, and continue my struggle toward recovery.

CONCLUSION
Manhattan, New York
A Sermon Given By
Rev. James Hayes S.S.S., Pastor
St. Andrew's Catholic Church
Lower Manhattan

It has been years since that scary "Ash" Tuesday morning in September. For most of us who live or work in the lower Manhattan area it appears as if it had happened yesterday. We who were here on that day and witnessed the horror, the chaos and the panic have not vanished. Memories creep into our minds like a bad dream. The images remain, like a personal video recording, which plays and replays in our psyches when we least expect it.

Within hours, evil men created a terror so close to our very soul. They have changed all of us on many unseen levels. However, while there are vivid memories of that madness, we also witnessed the best of the human spirit. Ordinary people helped others, risking life and limb to make a stranger safe. We saw courage that day and each day since the attack. We have heard the stories of the heroes. We have seen and cried over the pictures. We can recall many of those street corner shrines with pictures of the missing that have sprung up all over the city. We heard the constant testimony concerning lives that were taken. The small biographies in the papers, faces and histories, are recorded so that we may know whom this city has lost. Many of those lost were heroes in their respective communities even before the attack on the Towers. New York's finest and bravest also suffered much. They are our heroes. The task of obtaining closure for these families and all the families continues and appears to be endless. Individually and collectively, we have tried to obtain some closure by attending memorial and funeral services. We have stood side by side with grieving widows, children, and family members. The nearly 3,000 missing souls – sons and daughters, mothers and fathers – are New York's families and, more intimately, a part of our very own.

Initially, many tried to heal in a more formal setting. Many sought counseling immediately after the attack and still continue to process the pain. Many residents sought refuge outside the city. They perhaps hoped that by leaving the city, the memory of the events would vanish. Many residents also were forced to leave the area to take up temporary shelter outside the city. These displaced families walked the streets of lower Manhattan with bags and luggage like refugees fleeing before a war breaks out. Canal Street was the physical barrier. Below Canal Street, this area appeared like a military compound. The immediate evacuation of the area placed many families in a state of limbo months after that Tuesday morning. Our neighborhood was evacuated. There were no phones, no television, and there was this feeling of not knowing what building down here was going to be the next target. It was a very scary time. Needless to say, we here at St. Andrew's did not evacuate. We stood our ground knowing the danger that we faced by staying in the area.

Since the attack, many from this community have filled houses of worship. On the day of the attack many sought asylum here. We opened the basement to those who were wounded and needed shelter. Prayer services, processions, and other formal liturgical expressions of healing have filled the past years. There were memorial services, benefit concerts, fundraisers on all diverse levels. Truly, we have tried to heal in every manner imaginable. Yet, we know that healing is both a collective and individual journey.

Our neighborhood has become a shrine for tourists and the faithful who mourn. They come to take photos, place cards or flowers near the site, and silently pray. St. Paul's Chapel was adorned with countless messages of support from around the world. People seem to desperately want to catch a glimpse of Ground Zero – to make the history part of their reality. Others use this tragedy to sell NYPD or FDNY caps, packages of photos, and reminders of the Twin Towers. The selling of photos so near to the Towers really is somewhat obscene and out of place.

Reality for us has become too much. Even in our conversations we still speak of the "before" and the "after" of 9/11. Each day as we walk around and look up to the skyline, we feel a sense of absence – those gigantic Towers are really missing. Even among the many rescue workers, the Towers were first called the "pile" and later referred to simply as "the pit". For many though, it is still sacred ground. This day will be a psychological marker like the day when President Kennedy was shot. It became a psychic reference point of life up until that tragedy.

When we look at the sky the Towers, are missing. When we look up in the sky and see space only space, we are instantly transported back to that terrible Tuesday morning. The only structure that still remains standing is the Cross. It was found in the rubble of Tower 7 by an ironworker named Frank Lizzaro. It was he who spray painted in orange paint for the rescue workers arrows directing them to simply "God's House". It finally emerged from the rubble on the night of September 22, 2001. It will be part of the permanent Memorial.

The fire and the smoke continued to blanket the area for months. Initially, the rescue personnel worked feverishly on the "pile". There was always the hope that some one, any one, could be found alive. Those hopes were dashed. In early November, there was a change from Rescue of victims to Recovery. It was perhaps providential that those orders came down to the workers on the Feast of All Souls.

We had been able to get through the sixth month marker of September 11. A memorial at the base of Ground Zero commemorated the date. Our "new" mayor, at that point, spoke of moving forward and hinted about "getting on" with our lives. Many of us thought it was still too soon for that type of chatter. Despite most reports, a sense of normalcy is still a long way off. The city has been both blessed and cursed. We have been cursed with the excruciating pain of death and blessed with what was denied the victims: continuing life.

At seven o'clock, that same Sunday evening, two beams of light rose from above Ground Zero like a benediction, or a blessing. The Tribute in Light extended a mile into the night sky and deep into our hearts.

It lit the dark corners of our spirit enshrouded in grief. I must confess that I felt drawn to take a look and see how this memorial would affect me. Naturally, there was a sense of tremendous personal loss.

That week, in the <u>Wall Street Journal</u>, there were reports by several psychologists who were dealing with clients suffering from post-September 11th trauma. They warned that the "sixth-month marker" would be critical for many. Only now do suppressed emotions start to surface. For some it may mean that they can finally cry, for others it arrived as a sense of unrelenting despair. We native New Yorkers pride ourselves on our sophistication and strength, yet there was nothing that could have prepared us for this terrible tragedy. We were comforted by the fact that we are not alone in our anger, our vulnerability, or in our lingering sense of loss.

On that Sunday a hotly debated television show aired on CBS. The documentary, simply entitled, "9/11", began as the story of a rookie fireman but turned into a chronicle of the tragedy as witnessed by the members of the Duane Street firehouse, just a short block away from the Church. I confess that I did start watching the video. I had to shut it off when I heard an all too familiar sound. I recall that as I was ministering to the wounded in front of the Millennium Hotel. I had thought that I heard shots of gunfire coming from the Towers. I then heard the sound on the tape. It was not gunfire. It was the distinct sound of bodies falling to the earth. The sound resembled a bullet shot in the distance. I was brought right back to that day. I had to shut the television off. For some the video had re-opened scarcely healed wounds suffered that day. For those who did not bear eyewitness, the film was a testimonial to the bravery and selflessness displayed that fateful day.

The Towers of Light bore witness to the Towers of strength exemplified in the goodness of humankind. Each night we looked toward the vacant space in the sky where the Towers stood. We glanced at the two Towers of Light and absorbed what they symbolized. They were not a temporary replacement for the buildings that proudly stood there, but rather a tribute to so many bright, shining lives. They represented the personal torches that each New Yorker carries – hope and determination. At their highest point the twin beams converged just as the living and those who have passed on become one indomitable spirit. The lights had reached up to the heavens. Many, throughout the country, had thought the lights were a beautiful gesture. For most of us though, it was another painful reminder of what was missing. It was too early. A month later, in April, the lights vanished from the skyline. Our hearts were tugged, our memory reawakened. It appears now to have been cruel. Our spirit was lifted and then snuffed out like a candle.

The area checkpoints had crystallized the fact that we will perhaps never be the same. The re-routing of pedestrian walkways, the barricades, and picture identification were necessity for going from one point to another. Disaster centers were still open and staffed by the Red Cross, Safe Horizons, FEMA and other governmental agencies. The lines were not as long as they were immediately after the disaster. There was still endless talk in the press about the monies collected by these various organizations and criticisms over how they were being allocated. Local schools reopened for yet another school year. There were also stories decrying the "acceptable results" of the ongoing air quality tests. Buildings in lower Manhattan were all being cleaned. Some perhaps will also have to be demolished. As expected, conflicting reports exist about the quality of the air; one agency says one thing and another contradicts those findings and so on. Who can we trust? Alerts of new trouble afoot seem to haunt us. When will it end? Our lives have been turned upside down, and the process of getting back to a sense of normal is very arduous. Part of our very soul has been snatched from within us. Not a day goes by that we are not reminded.

Reports state that the city is "coming back" and recovering. There is much talk of rebuilding the Towers and constructing an appropriate memorial. There have been proposals and plans submitted.

New York is better now. Yet, I am still not too sure about its people. I hope that those who witnessed the horror and were part of the rescue/recovery effort simply don't relegate themselves to a permanent sense of sadness. We will heal and the sadness will become part of that journey.

The final day of the recovery operation on the site was very moving. On May 30, the last beam was cut from the "pit". In stark contrast to the chaos and horror of that "Ash Tuesday" months before, the silence of the ceremony spoke louder than any explosion. The last beam was lifted and was silently escorted from Ground Zero. As if in a funeral procession, the beam was draped in the American flag. The workers from all the uniformed services acted as escorts. There was a deep sense of reverence. The silence was dignity! It was a moment that tugged at America's heart. There were no speeches. Just the march from the site appeared to end one stage of our grieving process. As the ceremony continued, Brother Thomas and I watched it on television with the "brothers" from the Duane Street firehouse. Families, who had lost a firefighter or a loved one, gathered in the larger community of firefighters to simply gain comfort in being with America's heroes. It was a day to be with others rather than isolated and alone. Most of us simply want our own sense of life back, even though we may know consciously that it will never be the same. We wanted it to all disappear like a bad dream or a horrific nightmare. There is a need for us here in this area to gain some semblance of closure. I honestly think that closure is a very long way off. Spiritual, psychological, and emotional scars exist that can be reopened by the mere sound of an airplane flying close overhead. (Airplanes still appear lower in the sky these days.) We, as a people, have to come back to a sense of self. Maybe what I have realized is the very basic fact that each of us is a victim. Like soldiers in mortal combat, we are also suffering from post-traumatic stress. We have not yet found an appropriate space inside ourselves to place the horrific things we have seen.

Some have consulted psychologists or other mental health professionals in an effort to put words to the feelings that are still hidden. The process of verbalizing those terrible emotions is very painful. I recall attending a small prayer service after the tragedy. On the small table in the center of everything were sheets with just the names of the missing. I will never forget seeing all the names on those sheets.

Many have joined groups wherein their shared experiences make them feel that they are not alone in this solitary journey. I suppose I have realized that this feeling of trauma will never go away completely. It will perhaps become an easier burden to carry with each passing day. It is definitely a process. I don't think that we are quite there yet. There will be reminders and we will be shaken. We simply have to realize that it is okay! This is our healing process.

A report in late August 2002, expressed the fact that there have been 11 million visitors to Ground Zero between January and June. A recent map even has a shaded area where the Towers once stood overshadowing lower Manhattan. In its place is simply "Ground Zero."

As I am writing, September is arriving. We are planning memorials and prayer services. We here at the Church were too close that day. Perhaps we can never forget! We can never forget. Yet, I do hope that we will not be reminded so much and so often. This also is part of our process of healing. It is not the loud sounds that rattle our soul. It is not the sound of the low-flying aircraft that continue to make us pause and listen intensely. It is the small things of life that stop us cold. It is those private moments when something will trigger a memory, a situation, or a passing thought and we will shed a tear.

Part of the healing process is to continue to tell our own stories. It is a way of sharing our experience with others so that all of our pain can be attached to w.ords. The words can thereby also place names to the emotions and feelings buried within our souls and psyches. It is so painful.

As the day of Ash Tuesday approaches, it does not seem that all this time has passed. The difficulty here also lies in the fact that we who live here in this area are constantly reminded of the absence of the Twin Towers.

I think that by our prayers, by continuing to share our story with another, a Greater Wisdom will guide our halting steps. It will take a long time to heal.

(Endnotes)

[1] Information from David Sinclair – Spirit Cruises – New York
[2] Information from David Sinclair. – Spirit Cruises – New York
[3] Information from David Sinclair – Spirit Cruises – New York

This book is not endorsed by the Red Cross

Printed in the United States
55210LVS00006B/163-264